D/2013/45/360 - ISBN 978 94 014 0739 7 – NUR 793

Cover design: Lionel Schneider
Interior design: Peer De Maeyer

LannooCampus Publishers is a subsidiary of Lannoo Publishers,
the book and multimedia division of Lannoo Publishers nv

LannooCampus Publishers
Erasme Ruelensvest 179, box 101
3001 Leuven
Belgium
www.lannoocampus.be

CREDIT INSURANCE

WHAT IS IT?
WHY DO YOU NEED IT?
WHAT CAN IT DO FOR YOUR BUSINESS?

Paul Becue

In association with
EULER HERMES
Our knowledge serving your success

LANNOO CAMPUS

ACKNOWLEDGEMENTS

In the United Kingdom and Ireland Euler Hermes is the market leader in Credit Insurance as well as in Bonding. Being the authority in both fields, a number of our recent and former staff contributed to the launch of this English version. I would especially like to thank Terry Bridgman, ex-Head of Reinsurance of Euler Hermes in the UK. Terry spent considerable time on this book and has done a remarkable job in adapting it to the UK market.

A big thank you also to the following team at Euler Hermes in the UK that were of great assistance in making this edition happen:

Stephen Birmingham
Helen Taylor
Shaun Christian
Julie Roper
Daniel Gill
Angela Thompson
Helen Clark
Peter Evola
Silvia Gualda
Clive Hall-Strutt
Arabella Warden

Through this book we hope credit insurance will be introduced to a wider audience.

GERARD VAN KAATHOVEN
Euler Hermes United Kingdom & Ireland
Chief Executive Officer

FOREWORD

When the economy is going well, the sky is the limit for many companies. But when the economic cycle slips into a downward spiral, suppliers of goods and services run a significantly increased risk that their customers or 'buyers' will not be able to pay their bills, with the domino effect that even their own business may be threatened. The economic crisis, in which we still find ourselves in, has brought us all back down to earth – with more than one bump. The business community has been shaken to its very foundations.

Companies should apply the principle that they should only take calculated risks. This means covering those risks they are unable to influence, but which could nonetheless have a strong negative impact on their operational results. In other words, they need to be insured. Interest rate and FX risks have been covered in this manner for many years by many companies. Property and casualty insurance is also an everyday part of private and commercial life. However, credit insurance, the insurance of risks relating to the possible default of debtors, is still an area that is relatively unknown to the business community in the UK and Ireland. Research has shown consistently that companies cannot predict the majority of failures to which they are exposed. A £100m turnover business earning a 5% margin would have to increase its turnover by 20% to recoup a bad debt of £1m.

What we saw at the beginning of the crisis was a frequency issue – high volumes of smaller companies failing. What we are now seeing is a reduced number of failures, but larger in size.

Credit insurance supports sustainable growth by helping companies make informed decisions about the level of credit they should offer their customers, identifying those businesses at risk and enabling them to manage their credit risk exposure accordingly, avoiding the negative impact of unexpected bad debts or the need to make a claim. This ensures that companies are offering competitive credit to the right customers, converting opportunities into sales and profits. Like any other insurance policy the real proof comes if and when a claim needs to be made.

Should the unexpected happen and if a (larger) customer goes insolvent with no visible warning signs, through prompt payment of a claim, credit insurance offers peace of mind and security that a company can continue to trade without denting a company's profits.

Back in 2008, Paul Becue - the general manager of the information company of Euler Hermes in Belgium - published a detailed reference book about credit insurance: *Handboek Kredietverzekering. De Onzichtbare Bank* ('Credit Insurance. The Invisible Bank'). He followed this up with a handy and in many ways more accessible sequel, which explained in simple terms exactly how credit insurance operates. However, this book was specifically written for the Belgian market. For this reason, we have decided to make an English 'translation' of this excellent work, with an amended text more suitable to the conditions and practices found in the UK.

Credit insurance is essentially a homogenous product, which can be applied worldwide. However, many countries have added their own nuances to this basic product. For example, there are differences between the way credit insurance is implemented in France, Germany and the United Kingdom. There are also operational differences between the various credit insurance companies active in the market. When you are reading this book, you may even find it necessary to add nuances based on your own perspective. Nevertheless, our purpose was to write a manual in which the essential features of credit insurance are described in easy-to-understand language, without taking into account the details of every possible local variation. Paul Becue has succeeded admirably in this task.

Let us hope that in the coming years we will not forget the lessons of the recent past – it would be foolish to do otherwise.

I wish you an enjoyable and an informative read.

GERARD VAN KAATHOVEN
Euler Hermes United Kingdom & Ireland
Chief Executive Officer
www.eulerhermes.co.uk

CONTENTS

INTRODUCTION

During the financial and economic crisis of 2008-2009, credit insurance featured regularly in the news – and not always in a positive light (such as when cover was withdrawn for future transactions with a buyer, when that buyer was in major financial difficulty). Some criticisms were better founded than others, but generally they were wide of the mark. Most often, they arose because credit insurance suffers from being relatively unknown to the media and the wider public. It was only too easy therefore to concentrate on 'what happened' without understanding 'why it happened.' And as the old saying goes: 'unknown is unloved'. Consequently, it is important that credit insurers, beyond selling their products to individual companies, should make greater efforts to publicise more widely how valuable their cover can be and the role it plays in the broader economic community.

This will involve demonstrating how a company can use credit insurance to its maximum advantage. It will mean showing in detail how a credit insurance policy works. It will include explaining why companies should provide a credit insurer with the (often sensitive) information requested. This book attempts to shed some light on all these issues.

But we should be under no illusions. Credit insurance is a technical product and for this reason, we cannot avoid the use of technical terms. Nevertheless, it is intended to keep things as uncomplicated as possible. In this process, extensive reference will be made to charts and examples that are used within Euler Hermes, the world's leading credit insurer with an AA-rating.

This book focuses on the use of private credit insurance to provide cover against the credit risks involved in commercial, non-retail transactions, usually up to a maximum period of one year. This would be the case, for example, when a supplier delivers goods to a company based at home or overseas and has agreed payment terms involving a defined period of credit. We need to distinguish clearly between this type of private credit insurance and the credit and/or political risk insurance provided by the state, which works more to support the provision of medium or long term financing, relevant to major overseas capital goods contracts, projects and investments. The issuing of this type of export credit, bond support or investment guarantee is handled by governmental export credit agencies, in support of their country's export effort but within a framework of terms prescribed by international treaty agreements (this framework is designed to prevent an uncontrolled credit race). In the UK the public credit insurer is the ECGD.

The book is divided into five parts, of which parts II and IV are particularly important. In part II, we describe the technical operation of a credit insurance policy and explain how the credit insurer analyses the risk of default. In part IV, we take a look at the financial issues at stake from the point of view of the insured supplier and the importance of credit insurance in a wider economic context. By setting credit limits for buyers, terms of payment and amounts of debt, the credit insurer indirectly exercises a significant influence on the liquidity of the business community.

To a large extent, this book can be seen as a reworking of a book, I wrote some time ago (*Het handboek kredietverzekering. De onzichtbare bank:* The handbook of credit insurance. The invisible bank). The target audience for this first book (published by Intersentia) was the credit insurance sector, banks, legal practices, larger companies and the academic world in Belgium, but also the Netherlands. This present book is aimed at a wider, more international audience, whilst at the same time staying geared to the needs of smaller, non-retail companies. This means that close attention will be paid to the more essential and practical aspects of credit insurance available from the private market. Public credit insurance and judicial matters will only be touched on briefly.

The book is written in easily understandable language, with as little jargon as possible. The hope is that it will contribute towards a better understanding of credit insurance and improved communication between the credit insurance sector and the world of business generally. Credit insurance has a major influence on business liquidity, and ignorance of this fact can sometimes lead to frustrations in the business community. This book will go some way towards avoiding this problem in the future.

PAUL BECUE

PART 1

Definition and environment

In chapter 1, we define credit insurance and examine its most important principles. In chapter 2 we will explore the economic context. In chapter 3 we analyse the role of credit management within a company: above all, credit insurance must be viewed as an outsourced provider of support, for many of its functions.

CHAPTER 1
DEFINITION AND POSITIONING

1 What is (private) credit insurance?

In terms of European legislation, credit insurance falls under class 14 of the insurance sector. This section is simply known as 'credit'. Private credit insurance indemnifies sellers when trade receivables are not paid for by buyers, whether they are foreign and/or domestic. In other words, it covers the risk that can result from a loss caused by a buyer's insolvency or by his defaulting on an agreed debt. Insolvency is the legal or factual establishment of the financial incapacity of the debtor to pay his outstanding debts. In some countries and in some circumstances, the legal process necessary to obtain a formal declaration of insolvency may take a long time. In this event, subject to the debt being undisputed, credit insurance will normally consider claims under the protracted default cause of loss. In return for cover against these causes of loss, the insured customer pays a premium to the insurer. The cover is dependent on the insured customer having complied with all the conditions of the policy.

Assumption of risk on a buyer normally commences at the point of delivery of the goods and/or services. If the buyer goes 'bust' before the goods can be delivered, the goods can simply be re-sold elsewhere. However, manufacturers of tailor-made products (making them very difficult to re-sell in the event of a buyer's demise before delivery) can buy some protection against insolvency risks in this pre-delivery period.

The supplier of goods and/or services, who wishes to insure the risk of non-payment, therefore takes out a policy with a credit insurer. This policy will set out the terms and conditions on which cover will be given and sets a premium. Such conditions and premium are a reflection of the size and spread of the supplier's turnover, the trade sector and the historical experience of bad debts. The supplier's existing credit control systems are reviewed (e.g. what sources of information are used to check a buyer's creditworthiness; what standard actions are taken and when, in the event of non-payment by the due date). Subject to

GOOD TO KNOW

The buyer or debtor has a special status. There is no commercial or contractual relationship whatsoever between the insurer and the debtor: this relationship exists solely between the insured supplier and his buyer/debtor. The credit insurer's only contractual relationship is with the insured supplier. We shall see, however, that the actions of the credit insurer can have an impact on the liquidity and behaviour of the debtor, notwithstanding the absence of any direct commercial relationship between them.

the credit insurer being comfortable with his review, an agreed level of discretion will be granted to the supplier to approve credit limits up to a maximum amount, without further reference to the credit insurer. As a standard condition, the credit insurer will insist upon the insured supplier retaining a share of any loss for his own account. Thus, the indemnity offered will normally be 90% of the policyholder's loss. Any credit limit on a buyer above the agreed level of discretion has to be submitted to the credit insurer for specific approval.

FIGURE 1.1 *The relationship between the credit insurer and other third parties (source: Euler Hermes).*

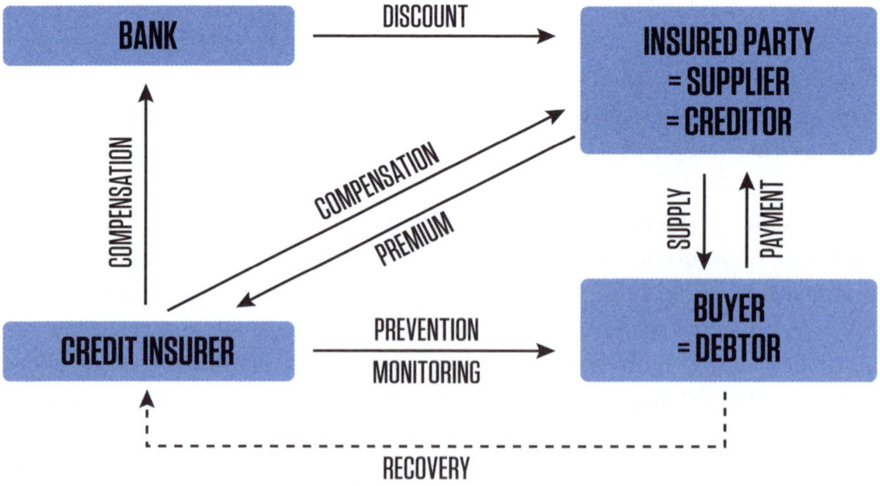

ATTENTION!

It is essential for all parties that the debtor is clearly identified, both for the insured supplier in terms of his contractual relationship and for the insurer who may acquire the rights of the insured party (a form of subrogation) after payment of the compensation has been made. The insurer will then attempt to recover this compensation from the debtor. This aspect of 'identification' is not found, for example, in theft insurance: in this case, the insurer also has a claim after the payment of compensation, but it is a claim against someone whose identity will probably never ascertained.

In figure 1.1, the bank enters the scenario as a possible third party. Banks provide credit to companies in the form of advances on a current account; for example, through the pre-financing of outstanding trade receivables for which the due date of payment has not yet been reached. As a security, the bank can demand that the company takes out a credit insurance policy, with the eventual payment of any loss compensation being allocated to the bank.

2 Three core tasks

The credit insurer has to recognise that there will be no business to insure, unless the insured customers (the suppliers) are able to generate sales. However, the insured customer has to recognise that unless the buyer pays for the goods/services supplied, those sales will result in a loss. It is on the back of this reconsidered partnership that the credit insurer will work with his insured customer to achieve three objectives:

- Prevention: Every credit case is assessed on the creditworthiness and the ability of the buyer to pay. These factors are then monitored continuously. Credit limits are calculated as the maximum balance that will be outstanding for payment at any one time. The ideal objective, for both parties, is to be able to agree what is required, in order to achieve the desired level of sales. Lower limits than ideally required obviously impact on the supplier's negotiations with his buyer.
- Indemnity: Payment of claims when a buyer with an agreed credit limit (including one set under the insured supplier's discretionary limit) fails to pay.

- Recovery: The credit insurer will attempt to achieve recovery of any loss of payments by co-joining with his insured supplier to pursue the buyer for the outstanding debt. (This might, for example, mean taking legal action to ensure the buyer pays or it might mean arranging a payment plan whereby the buyer pays off the debt over time.)

3 What is insolvency?

In view of these core tasks, insolvency of the debtor is one of the most relevant issues for the credit insurer. This gives the insured supplier the right to receive indemnity on the basis of the financial inability of the debtor to meet its obligations. A company may be considered insolvent if it is unable to pay its debts as they fall due or if its assets are insufficient to discharge its liabilities.

Section 123 of the UK Insolvency Act 1986 sets out when a company is deemed unable to pay its debts (i.e. technically insolvent) and it includes failure to comply with a statutory written demand for a debt exceeding £750 or with a judgment enforcement order, or if the value of the company assets is less than its liabilities.

In the context of credit insurance, insolvency covers a wide range of procedures, which include rescue mechanisms such as administration, schemes of arrangement or a CVA (company voluntary arrangement), and a liquidation which results in the company being wound up and dissolved:

- **Administration**: the main aim of this procedure is to rescue or restructure the company, in order to achieve a better outcome for creditors than might be achieved by liquidation. The administrator is court-appointed and has a duty to act on behalf of all creditors.
- **Administrative receivership**: an administrative receiver is appointed by the holder of a floating charge and acts on behalf of the charge holder, rather than all creditors. This procedure can only be used for floating charges invoked prior to 15 September 2003, when the Enterprise Act was introduced. Exceptionally, some more complex financial transactions, such as those relating to public service companies, still allow for administrative receiverships in all cases.
- **Company voluntary arrangement**: this is the only procedure that allows a debtor to retain legal control over the company, under the supervision of an Insolvency practitioner. This is a collective procedure between the company

and its creditors, which generally requires that part of the debts are relinquished in order to allow the company to continue operations. Agreement on the part of the creditors is required.

- **Liquidation:** this procedure is most commonly used when a company cannot be rescued. The company ceases trading and its assets are realised. The liquidator can be appointed by the company, its shareholders or creditors. The liquidator acts on behalf of all creditors and has powers of investigation extending to the conduct of the directors of the business.

In recent years in the UK there has been a significant growth in the number of 'pre-pack' administrations. These occur when a sale of the profitable assets of an insolvent company is agreed in private through advisers (often with the agreement of the secured creditors), before the company formally enters administration, and without the involvement of the court or a creditors' committee. The advisers are then appointed as administrators, and the sale is immediately completed. Such deals have been the subject of criticism, particularly where the sale is to a party connected to the original owners of the company, because unsecured trade creditors (whose debts are usually eliminated entirely) have no opportunity to influence the process, and cannot always be sure that the transaction has been carried out in their best interests.

4 General principles

4.1 INSURING THE TRADE DEFAULT RISK

As we have seen, the purpose of credit insurance is to provide insurance cover to suppliers against the risk of non-payment for goods and/or services supplied on credit terms. This is the commercial risk. The emphasis is on trade credit in transactions conducted between businesses, and not on sales to individuals. Sole traders can be considered for credit insurance, though they may need to meet specific criteria; e.g comply with the terms of the Companies Act of

GOOD TO KNOW

Credit insurance therefore operates in a business-to-business (B2B) environment. The insured parties are companies, not individuals.

2006 (substitution of section 1201) and the subsequent Regulations of 2009. Non-profit organisations also fall outside the core activities of the credit insurer, since these organisations do not carry out a commercial activity.

Normally, buyers who are state or municipal departments also fall outside the scope of credit insurance cover, since they are deemed to be unable to become insolvent. Contracts with such organisations, within the EU or OECD, need not be declared to the credit insurer. However, contracts with public sector organisations elsewhere in the world may be considered open to the risk of cancellation or non-payment for reasons that are more political than financial. In this case a supplier may consider widening the scope of his credit insurance cover to include political risks. Political risk cover can be taken against the risk that contracts become frustrated by a range of events beyond the control of the buyer and seller (for example: wars, revolutions, etc.); or by economic difficulties, such as a shortage of foreign currency leading to long delays in transferring money; or the imposition of new laws that effectively prevent financial performance.

4.2 INSURING THE GLOBAL TURNOVER OF THE COMPANY

In most cases, a company will be offered a whole turnover policy. The underlying philosophy is that the credit insurer wishes to prevent the insured party from making a systematic selection of risks, so that only the worst of these risks are insured. This is related to the general principle of a sound and balanced spread of risk (mutualisation), on which the insurance world as a whole is based. The provision of cover for 'one-off' risks does sometimes happen, but it is very rare.

WHAT YOU NEED TO KNOW

In principle, the insured supplier's global turnover must be offered for cover to the credit insurer. Obviously, some exclusions are possible (such as the public sector contracts mentioned above), but generally the greater the level of selection being offered, the less acceptable the risk becomes to the insurer.

4.3 THE CREDIT INSURER'S ROLE IN AGREEING BUYER RISKS

The credit insurer not only removes risk from his customer, he also plays a preventative role. This latter function is most important; it is the means by which the insurer offers support to the insured supplier's own credit management policy and practices. Whilst there is a recognition that it is sometimes necessary to take and accept risks in order to succeed – and make a profit – those risks have to be considered acceptable.

Each new request for credit insurance therefore involves a financial analysis of the default risk and, when appropriate, the agreement of a credit limit. If a limit is issued, the risk is systematically monitored. If there is any question of a deterioration in the creditworthiness of the debtor, the credit limit can be reduced or withdrawn for future deliveries. There will inevitably be consultation with the supplier at this point as to the best way to proceed. When a buyer is in danger of going under, he is normally unconcerned about not increasing his debt any further and not taking further deliveries. However, in some circumstances when this is not the case, the credit insurer and supplier will work together, and, if necessary, with the buyer, to find a solution. Obviously, no credit insurer will retain credibility if he withdraws cover without full consideration of all of the facts. He only takes such drastic action when the available information is so adverse as to force his hand.

If a supplier has taken the option to cover the pre-delivery risk in his policy, then the credit insurer knows full-well that he is likely to be at risk for all existing contracts, should a limit need to be withdrawn.

MISUNDERSTANDING

It is sometimes assumed that credit insurers must accept all risks under the terms of a whole turnover policy, even the bad ones. This is not the case. The premium rate for the policy, and other terms and conditions, are indeed set on the basis that the insured party will be offering his whole turnover for inclusion in the policy. But underwriting judgment as to individual buyer credit limits is separate and is part of the support given to a company's own credit management systems.

4.4 INDEMNIFYING THE INSURED PARTY

Notwithstanding the efficient monitoring of the accepted credit risks, claims requiring the payment of indemnity for loss will still occur. No one can foresee all future circumstances and events. Who, for example, would have thought that the banks of the Western World teetered on the verge of insolvency in the autumn of 2008? While the purpose of the insurer's preventative role is to avoid as many insolvencies as possible, when a default does occur the credit insurer will pay the indemnity to the insured party for his loss.

GOOD TO KNOW

The real added value of a credit insurer is to support each individual policyholder by bringing to bear not only his skills in financial analysis, but also his wide ranging experience within trade sectors and the spread of knowledge from his overall client portfolio.

4.5 PARTICIPATION OF THE INSURED PARTY

In principle, a credit insurer never provides 100% cover. Generally, the insured indemnity is 90% of the risk. This means that a claim for £ 1,000 as a result of a business failure will lead to the payment of compensation amounting to £ 900. By insisting that the insured party retains an interest in the debt, the credit insurer wishes to ensure that the insured will also monitor the default risks carefully and, where necessary, assertively. Experience has shown that the granting of 100% cover nearly always reduces the insured party's willingness and enthusiasm to follow up matters (especially in taking recovery action). It is therefore appropriate within the shared responsibility and 'partnership' between the credit insurer and the insured supplier that the latter should also be obliged to carry part of the risk.

GOOD TO KNOW

It is usually stipulated in the policy as a matter of principle that the insured supplier cannot insure his 10% participation elsewhere.

4.6 THE OPTION TO ASSIGN THE BENEFITS OF THE POLICY

The assigning of the benefits of a policy means that any loss due may be paid to the third party to whom the assignment was made, probably a bank. The trade receivables asset in a balance sheet may represent a significant proportion of the company's total assets. If that asset is to be used, in whole or in part, as security for bank borrowing, then the credit insurance policy can be used to enhance that security.

ATTENTION!

The policy benefits can be transferred to a third party for the provision of additional financing security. The credit insurer must agree to this transfer in writing, in order to prevent double-financing of the same debt.

5 How public credit insurance is different

Private credit insurance is entirely focussed on trade-related transactions. Whilst the main focus of public credit insurers is similar, it should be recognised that they and some other private sector insurers also provide cover against confiscation, expropriation and nationalisation risks (in the UK known as CEND), when overseas investments are made. The national export credit agencies (see 5.2 below) also offer financial guarantees and bond support cover in long-term deals (e.g. ships and aircraft).

In this book, however, the focus is on short term commercial trading transactions.

5.1 PRIVATE CREDIT INSURANCE: SHORT TERM

Private credit insurance relates to cover for default and risk of non-payment in respect of debtors, who within the framework of trade transactions (the purchase of goods and services) have been granted credit terms (i.e. a postponement of payment) by their suppliers. Worldwide, this credit insurance market is dominated by three large groups: Euler Hermes, Atradius and Coface.

Historically, private credit insurance companies operated as domestic credit insurers purely within their own domestic economies. Gradually, however, since the 1970's the scope of business has been extended to cover first commercial default risks in exporting to OECD (Organisation for Economic Cooperation and Development) countries and then credit and political risks when exporting all over the world. With increasing globalisation, it is now even possible for international groups of companies (with subsidiaries operating in different countries) to place their credit insurance cover with a single credit insurer.

5.2 PUBLIC CREDIT INSURANCE: MEDIUM AND LONG TERM

Public credit insurance relates to the cover provided by export credit agencies (ECAs). These bodies are sometimes an arm of government itself (e.g. the Export Credit Guarantee Department (ECGD) in the United Kingdom), or insurance companies that are 100% owned by government for the sole purpose of supporting that country's own export effort (e.g. the Belgian National Delcredere Service), or commercial companies given a state guarantee for a specific 'ring-fenced' part of their operation (e.g. Euler Hermes in Germany, NCM in the Netherlands, now part of the Atradius Group, and Coface in France).

The main aim of the state provision of credit or investment insurance is to support local industries in their drive to increase exports. Some level of manufacturing support may also be provided, as can support for bonding requirements ('bond support'), linked to an insured contract. Within the framework of the OECD, a number of agreements exist to restrict public subsidy and unbridled competition between the different member countries with regard to the length of credit that may be provided and, indeed, the type of risks that can be covered in competition with the private sector.

Because state intervention is involved, these ECAs offer intensive support first and foremost to their own exporters, who are registered and pay tax in their own local national markets. Although the public credit insurance market has been undergoing rapid change in recent years as a result of increasing globalisation, the most noticeable effect has been in the consolidation of the private credit insurance market. As we said in Section 5.1, private credit insurers have been extending their activities globally (including the acceptance of political risks), and are also becoming more active in the field of long-term cover. As the boundaries between public and private credit insurance has become more and more blurred, so the European Commission has moved to counteract the perceived distortion of the competition between the two sectors and has issued a number of Notifications, relating to the distinction between marketable risks and non-marketable risks. Marketable risks are those where capacity is regularly available in the insurance and reinsurance markets. Thus, it is considered unfair for governments to compete in a market whose needs can generally be met by the private sector. An example of this is that public credit insurers may not undertake to credit insure risks in certain countries (usually OECD countries) with a payment period of two years or less.

6 The credit insurance market: a niche in between the insurance and banking sectors

In legal terms, credit insurance in most countries is defined and regulated as part of the general class of 'Insurance':

- → European legislation classifies credit insurance under class 14 of the insurance sector.
- → As with other types of insurance, the insured party (supplier) pays a premium. In exchange for this, he receives cover against the risk of the possible payment default or insolvency of his customers. If this risk materialises in the form of defaulted payments, the credit insurer will pay the insured indemnity relating to the loss to the insured party.
- → As with other insurers, reserves must be set aside, based on actuarial and statistical calculations, in order to meet potential claims from insured suppliers.
- → The annual financial accounts must be drawn up in a specific manner, comparable to other insurance companies.
- → For the calculation of minimum capital and solvability requirements, the credit insurer is subject to the Solvency II regulations for the insurance sector (as opposed to the Basel II/III regulations for the banking sector).

On the other hand, it is also true that the credit insurer, by the very nature of his task (providing cover for insolvency risk), is involved de facto in the financial analysis of companies. In this respect, his credit analysts also act like those of a bank, with the difference being that the credit insurer places greater emphasis on the short term (in principle, up to one year), whereas a bank dealing with investment credit adopts a much more long-term perspective.

Other points of difference are:

- the credit insurer is not directly involved in funding;
- in general, the credit insurer does not hold guarantees in the same way as a bank; which as a manager of money originating from third parties must (in theory, at least) be perceived to be more cautious in its approach to credit risk. On the other hand, it should be noted that banks are, on the whole, covered by legal charges over the assets of the borrowing party, whereas credit insurers are generally unsecured, relying on up-to-date payment history and buyer information when making their credit assessments of the buyer risk. A credit insurer may also benefit from recoveries obtained from any retention of title.

For all these reasons, credit insurance has been able to create its own niche market.

7 Surety insurance: the mirror image of credit insurance?

Many credit insurance companies are also active in surety insurance, and both insurance branches are regularly treated together under legislation. This is due to the fact that surety insurance can, in a way, be considered as a kind of reverse credit insurance: instead of being paid by the supplier, the premium is paid by the buyer or debtor. The insured interest is the same in both cases: the payment of the trade receivable at due date on behalf of the supplier.

But surety insurance is more than this. Bonds, guarantees and indemnities all form part of the often complex arena of 'surety'. Surety bonds have been used for many centuries to 'guarantee' obligations, particularly between trading parties. References to surety bonds are also found in the writings of Shakespeare and the first corporate surety company was established in the UK in the 19th century.

A surety bond is a means of creating a form of security for the employer of a contractor or service provider, essentially creating a guarantee to compensate for losses and damages sustained as a result of a breach of contractual obligations or insolvency. Bonds are therefore a deed of guarantee rather than a contract of insurance. In most countries bonds can be provided by either major banking or insurance organisations. Bonds are provided and made available, on recourse terms only, where the guarantor's obligation is secondary to the primary obligation of the contractor/service provider under a contract. Unlike indemnity insurance (as with credit insurance), bond premiums are charged for the use of the surety's financial status and guarantee.

Generally, bonds fall into two broad classes:
- On-demand bonds: these can be called at the sole discretion of the employer and are payable at first request. Typically, these would be issued by banks, which do not wish to become involved in potential contractual disputes between the trading parties.
- Conditional bonds: these are bonds where loss or damage has to be ascertained and certified pursuant to the underlying contractual agreements. These would typically be used in support of local contract performance obligations, and are widely applicable to the construction industry.

Typical types of bonds and guarantees would include the contractual bonds:
- Bid or tender bonds: these are issued as part of a *bidding process* to the project owner, to guarantee that the winning bidder will undertake the *contract* as set out in the terms under which they made their bid;
- Performance bonds: these are issued to guarantee satisfactory completion of a project by a *contractor*;
- Advance payment bonds: these *provide* that the advanced *sum* will be returned if the *agreement* under which the *advance* was made cannot be fulfilled;
- Progress and stage payment bonds;
- Retention bonds.

In addition to these contractual guarantees, there are also the legal bonds:
- Customs bonds;
- License, permit or regulatory bonds.

Surety in different countries is characterised and strongly influenced by local laws, customs and markets. International surety companies, often involved in many lines of international insurance business, will have local specialist knowledge in the field of surety, as well as international expertise from the major insurance centres of the world.

CHAPTER 2
THE ECONOMIC CONTEXT AND OFFICIAL INSOLVENCIES

The economic cycle has a decisive impact on the payment behaviour of companies and, as a consequence, on the number of failures or insolvencies.

1 The Purchasing Manager's Index (PMI) as Europe's leading indicator.

The working of the credit insurance sector is dependent to a large extent on the prevailing economic climate, and in particular its macro-economic aspects.

This is expressed in the economic cycle, which is a reflection of the current economic conditions at any one time. Markit publishes on a monthly basis its Purchasing Manager's Index (PMI). Markit is a UK global financial information services company. Its PMI surveys are the most closely-watched business surveys in the world (website: *www.markiteconomics.com*), favoured by central banks and business decision-makers for their ability to provide up-to-date indicators of economic trends. The PMI survey is continually tracking variables such as output, new orders, stock levels, employment and prices across the manufacturing, construction, retail and service sectors. Figure 2.1 shows the PMI in the eurozone (i.e. without the UK) for global economic activity. The chart shows that the PMI surveys, which are a reflection of global business sentiment, are closely related to the GDP evolution. A PMI below 50 points towards an economic contraction (or negative GDP). Moreover, while most GDP figures are released after a delay on a quarterly basis, the PMI is quickly published on a monthly basis.

Credit insurance is a cyclical activity. During boom periods – when the economic cycle is favourable – the insured parties will suffer relatively little loss from insolvencies and the insurer will be required to pay less compensation.

FIGURE 2.1 *Markit Eurozone PMI (Purchasing Manager's Index) and GDP (Gross Domestic Product) (source: Markit, Eurostat)*

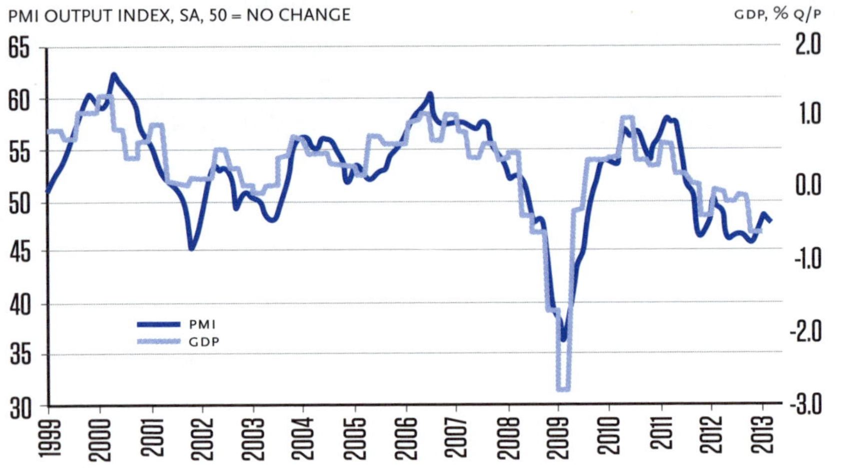

For the insurer, this leads to growing pressure to reduce the level of premiums and also means that for commercial reasons he will be compelled to accept more risks on potentially 'weak' debtors. When the economic cycle changes and the economic climate becomes less favourable, this can cause considerable problems for the insurer:

- The number of loss claims and the amount of compensation to be paid increases, but the level of premium does not initially rise to the same degree, even though this would be justified in terms of the greater risk now being run.
- Moreover, the turnover of most companies falls during a recession – and turnover is the basis for the calculation of the insurer's premiums, which therefore leads to further reduction in income.

This was the scenario that became a reality during the financial and economic crisis of 2008-2009.

In addition to effective economic growth, the level of growth in world trade is also a significant factor. Table 2.1 compares the growth in world GDP (gross domestic product) with the growth of world trade in goods and services on the basis of volume. A comparison based on the value of goods would probably have enhanced the results still further, in view of the strong rise in the price of raw materials during the period 2003-2006 and in 2010.

Table 2.1 also shows that in recent years world trade has grown faster than the production of goods and services based on world GDP. The only exception was the recession year of 2009. This, of course, is related to the increasing globalisation of the economy and the rise of China as an economic superpower. This is very important for the credit insurance sector, since credit insurers cover the risks associated with possible default in respect of trade receivables. With the growth in world trade, the number and value of trade receivables has also increased strongly.

TABLE 2.1 *Comparison of world GDP with the growth in the volume of world trade (change per year in %) (source: Euler Hermes)*

	World GDP	World trade
2007	+4.2%	+7.2%
2008	+1.9%	+2.6%
2009	-2.0%	-11.8%
2010	+4.2%	+13.9%
2011	+3.0%	+5.9%
2012	+2.4%	+3.5%
2013 (*)	+2.5%	+4.1%
2014 (*)	+3.2%	+5.9%

(*) Forecast

ATTENTION!

The longer the due dates for the settlement of accounts receivable, the greater the chance that the account in question will not be paid on the date due. This can threaten the continued existence of a company. Lack of payment discipline also has an impact on the profitability and cashflow of the creditor. Late settlement of debts puts a brake on economic growth and reduces productivity, because companies have fewer financial resources at their disposal to make necessary investments.

2 Payment behaviour

It is self-evident that in moments of a weak economic cycle companies will be inclined to settle their outstanding business debts less quickly than in boom periods.

A study by the Intrum Justitia debt collection agency in 2012 revealed that 55 % of the companies questioned admitted to suffering liquidity problems due to late payment. The survey also revealed the amount of debt being written off had grown to 2.8 % of total receivables, reaching the unprecedented level of 340 billion euros, a figure equal to the total debt of Greece or to one-third of total annual healthcare spending across the EU's 27 countries, or more than double the EU's total 2012 budget of 147 billion euro. These are indeed 'serious' amounts.

2.1 SMEs are the biggest victims

ATTENTION!

SMEs are particularly vulnerable in this respect, since they usually have only a limited financial base and liquidity. In these circumstances, an 'accident' in the shape of an unpaid account can have disastrous consequences.

According to a study by the European Commission in 2009, the annual turnover reflected in delayed accounts receivable amounted to 1,864 billion euros, almost two-thirds of which (1,141 billion euros) was owed to small and medium-sized enterprises. These SMEs are doubly vulnerable to the effects of late payment because:

- SMEs experience greater fluctuations in cash-flow; as a result, they frequently need to take out short-term credits to meet their cash-flow needs; however, they often have only limited access to such credits and they are expensive in terms of the interest payable;
- SMEs are frequently dependent for a large proportion of their turnover on a limited number of large customers; these customers can sometimes abuse their position as key accounts by delaying the settlement of invoices for an unacceptably long period;

→ the administrative costs of collecting outstanding debts are relatively high for SMEs; they do not have either the specialist personnel or the time to monitor these debts effectively.

In this context, credit insurance certainly offers added value to SMEs.

It was with the aim of offering help of this kind to SMEs that the European Commission issued a new Directive on 16 February 2011, specifically designed to combat late payment in commercial transactions (see below).

2.2 CULTURAL DIFFERENCES

→ *Countries and public authorities*

TABLE 2.2 *Payment behaviour in Europe in 2008 (source: European Commission; Intrum Justitia European Payment Index 2008)*

In days	B2B			Public authority		
	1	2	3	1	2	3
UK	**33.2**	**51.0**	**17.8**	**30.0**	**48.0**	**18.0**
Germany	30.0	36.0	6.0	25.0	40.0	15.0
France	49.0	65.0	16.0	57.0	71.0	14.0
Italy	68.0	88.0	20.0	95.0	135.0	40.0
Spain	73.0	89.0	16.0	103.0	144.0	41.0
Poland	29.7	46.8	17.1	27.7	47.9	20.2
Netherlands	26.1	40.0	13.9	27.2	46.0	18.8
Belgium	37.0	50.0	13.0	49.0	75.0	21.0

1 = Average duration – **2** = Average total duration – **3** = Delay

The European Commission has tried to improve these figures with the introduction of its Directive to combat late payment in commercial transactions. The Directive of 16 February 2011 was targeted first and foremost at public authorities, as this is the area with the most room for improvement. Table 2.2 shows clearly that government bodies are currently not setting a good example in this respect: in most countries they take longer to pay than their counterparts in the private sector. The reason for this is that, in some countries at least, by delaying payments in this manner it is often possible to make the national budget (which is usually drawn up on the basis of cash accounting) seem healthier than it really is.

In the past, companies and sectors that were heavily dependent on state subsidies tended to adopt the same approach: if they had to wait for money from the state, others would have to wait for money from them. If the Directive can persuade national governments to break with this bad habit, the result will be to provide the business community as a whole with greater financial room for manoeuvre. It is therefore important that governments should set a good example to others and should seek to stimulate a more 'moral' approach to correct payment between companies.

ATTENTION!

As far as the payment behaviour of companies is concerned, it is clear that there is a huge cultural difference between Northern Europe and Southern Europe. In Northern Europe the due dates for payment are much shorter and the number of days in arrears is significantly lower. In other words, there is much greater payment discipline. The mentality in Southern Europe is clearly different. Both the due dates for payment and the delays in complying with the due date are much longer. On this basis, it is possible to conclude that the risk of non-payment is greater in Southern Europe than it is in Northern Europe. But it is not a simple task to change this: late payment is deeply ingrained in the culture of these South European countries. As a result, these differences in payment behaviour can sometimes lead to competition distortion within the single market of the European Union.

→ *Sectors*

In addition to geographical differences, there are also behavioural differences between sectors. Companies that are active in sectors such as building, catering, business services, transport and agriculture are the least prompt settlers of outstanding invoices. Institutions and foundations also have a bad reputation in this respect.

Having said this, it is important to place matters in their proper perspective. For example, many of the disputes in the building sector are a result of the discussions held during the provisional completion and acceptance procedure for new building work.

→ *Foreign and domestic markets*

The risk of non-payment increases for companies who export goods to other countries within the European Union. For exporters trading with countries outside the Union, this risk is even greater. The transaction costs are higher as a result of the unreliable nature of the information and uncertainties relating to the market position and the solvency of debtors who do not operate in the domestic market.

ATTENTION!

The unreliability of information means that the buyer also runs a lower risk of damage to his reputation because of late payment when the creditor is located in another member state. In other words, reputational damage decreases as distance increases.

The costs for the provision of trade credit are much higher for exporting companies. The language and legislation are both different and access to solvency information is less complete. This increases the monitoring cost, while the chances of successfully enforcing payment are correspondingly lower.

2.3 THE REASONS FOR LATE PAYMENT

The first EC Directive to combat late payment in respect of commercial transactions, issued on 29 June 2000, foresaw the possibility to claim default interest on the basis of the reference rate published by the European Central Bank, increased with an additional margin of 7%. For various reasons, this has seldom happened – as can be seen from the details in table 2.3.

GOOD ADVICE

According to the European Commission, this is the reason why increasing use is being made of credit insurance and other instruments that help to manage trade risks. They reduce uncertainty relating to income, but they increase production costs by virtue of the necessity to pay the additional credit insurance premium, as well as costs associated with factoring, the purchase of trade information, debt collection, guarantees, etc. This can take a huge bite out of the company's profit margin, particularly for smaller enterprises.

TABLE 2.3 *Reasons for not claiming default interest, expressed in % (source: European Commission; IPM/International Policy Making; EBTP/European Business Test Panel)*

	IPM	EBTP
Fear of losing the customer	58.3	68.5
Procedures too complex to claim interest	47.9	45.9
Competition never demands interest on late payment	37.5	28.8
Default interest is regarded as income	4.9	13.5
Ignorance of the existence of the possibility to claim default interest	11.8	13.5
The rate of interest is unknown	7.6	7.2
Don't know	3.5	5.4

This partially explains the reasons for late payment on the part of the debtors and the relatively passive response on the part of the creditors. In this respect, the elements discussed hereunder are also relevant factors. The European Commission has admitted that it can exert little influence via new legislation on the first two of these elements – market structure and the economic cycle.

→ *Market structure*

The level of competition within a market, the relative power of the market participants and the associated fear of damaging customer relations are important factors. They determine whether or not creditors are prepared to accept late payment and whether or not debtors are likely to try and secure an extension of the payment period.

The most compelling reason for debtors to pay on time is the preservation of their professional and/or business reputation. On the other hand, they know that they are unlikely to be penalised for late payment, in part because the creditors do not want to damage their commercial relations and in part because the legal procedures are too long and too costly.

In general, SMEs are in the weakest bargaining position, particularly in their dealings with larger companies. To secure orders, they sometimes have to agree to long payment deadlines. SMEs often also lack the necessary time and expertise to negotiate contracts effectively. Consider, for example, the one-sided initiative of the brewery group AB Inbev in April 2009 to increase its payment date for its suppliers from 30 days to 120 days.

→ *The economic cycle*

It is easy to understand how a downturn in the economy can lead to an increase in payment arrears. Company turnover falls, with a corresponding decrease in cash-flow. Banks are also more careful about lending money during slumps. This has been plain for all to see since the start of the financial and economic crisis of 2008-2009.

However, a positive change in the economic climate can also result in an increase of payment arrears. Suddenly, the companies are presented with new opportunities for investment, for which they need to make maximum use of their available financial resources.

→ *Access to funding and budgetary limitations*

Monetary policy, liquidity levels and the availability of bank credit can also influence a company's payment behaviour. This is particularly the case for companies where bank credit is a substitute for supplier credit.

Budgetary problems at government level can also have a knock-on effect, resulting in the slower payment of outstanding accounts.

→ *The internal organisation of the debtors and creditors*

The creditor's own credit management procedures, coupled with the quality of their products and services, are important factors in helping to secure prompt payment. However, many SMEs do not possess effective credit management systems to either monitor or prevent delayed payment.

→ *A lack of efficient remedies*

Few companies pursue the option of claiming default interest, because the costs often outweigh the financial benefits. The additional paperwork that the default procedures involve is seldom translated into a net cash gain.

2.4 THE EUROPEAN DIRECTIVE 2011/7/EU OF 16 FEBRUARY 2011 ON COMBATING LATE PAYMENT IN COMMERCIAL TRANSACTIONS.

This new 2011 Directive replaced an earlier version issued in 2000. The 2000 Directive was often referred to as the 'Credit Management Directive', but initially few legislative initiatives were introduced in this domain. The purpose of the new Directive was to secure a degree of consistency in the payment periods adopted by the various member states, since the existing differences between countries were actually leading to unfair competition. In this way, it was hoped that the Directive will act as a form of support for the credit management carried out at company level.

The Directive of 29 June 2000 was the first important step taken at European level to secure the prompt and correct payment of trade receivables. Its provisions were only applicable to national and international transactions between companies or between companies and the government. The Directive was introduced by law in the different EU countries. However, there was little improvement at this stage – and this for three main reasons:

1. The contractual freedom of the individual parties to the business transaction remained paramount.
2. In the event of problems, the creditor was still more likely (for commercial reasons) to waive his right to claim default interest and the related costs: preserving the relationship with the debtor was more important.
3. The government's own payment behaviour set a poor example.

The new Directive 2011/7/EU works within the framework of the European Small Business Act, which aims to reduce the administrative burden on companies. An improved access to funding for SMEs and the development of a legislative and business framework that encourages prompt payment is regarded as one of the ten basic principles of SME policy in the European Union.

The EU now proposes that all invoices should be paid as a matter of principle within 30 days. This applies to both the public and private sectors. Every effort has been made to close potential loopholes, which might otherwise make delayed payment still possible (although this hasn't happened as yet):

- If both parties to a transaction are in agreement, the payment period can be extended to a maximum of 60 days. A longer period is also possible when this is expressly agreed between the creditor and the debtor, and provided that it is not grossly unfair to the creditor.
- Public authorities can also obtain an extended payment period, but this must be explicitly agreed in advance and must be capable of objective justification in relation to the nature and specific features of the contract in question. The European Parliament considers that this period should never be longer than 60 days. In this way, for example, public hospitals could take advantage of the 60 day rule, since they are largely financed on the basis of refunds through various social insurance mechanisms, which often take some time to complete.

In addition, there is also a so-called 'verification period' of 30 days, during which the buyer has the right to check that the goods and/or services provided are in accordance with the conditions set down in the contract of purchase. This period can also be extended, if it is possible to show that complex market conditions are involved (for example, in Italy and Germany), and again on condition that this is explicitly agreed in advance and is not grossly unfair to the creditor. The European Parliament is convinced that this verification period will not be used as an excuse to delay payments unnecessarily.

In the event that payment of an outstanding invoice is not made on time, the creditor has the right to claim default interest on the basis of the reference rate published by the European Central Bank, increased with an additional margin of 8% (instead of the 7% foreseen in the 2000 Directive). In addition, he can also claim minimum compensation for his collection costs in the form of a fixed fee of 40 euros.

As far as the retention of title is concerned (see chapter 11), very little has changed. It can be exercised in accordance with the relevant national provisions, which, according to international private law, are applicable in such circumstances.

In addition to this Directive, in recent years the European Union has also introduced a number of other Regulations, with the intention of simplifying the procedures for legal claims between member states, including the settlement of unpaid trade accounts. In the first instance, this related more specifically to the introduction in 2000 of the principle of the mutual recognition of legal decisions in respect of civil and commercial cases. This was followed in 2006 by a Regulation introducing the European payment order procedure. The preamble of this Regulation states that the swift and efficient recovery of outstanding debts over which no legal controversy exists is of paramount importance for the economic operators in the European Union, as late payments constitute a major reason for insolvency threatening the survival of businesses, particularly small and medium-sized enterprises, thereby resulting in numerous job losses.

2.5 CONSEQUENCES FOR COMPANY CASH-FLOW

The length of the payment period also has an influence on the financial structure of a company. The longer the average length of this period of outstanding payments (DSO = Days Sales Outstanding), the more heavily it weighs on the assets side of the company balance sheet. We shall see later that this has an important impact on the financing of the company's working capital.

During the preparatory phase of the new Directive 2011/7/EU, the European Commission carried out a number of simulated tests on the basis of the new maximum payment period of 30 days. The tests were confined to B2B transactions (transactions with government authorities were not included). The results for the most optimistic scenario (reduction of the payment period to 30 days and no arrears) showed a cash-flow or liquidity gain of 192.8 billion euros throughout the European Union. The gain for UK companies alone was estimated at 21.5 billion euros.

Even in a more realistic scenario (reduction of the payment period to 30 days and a reduction in the level of arrears proportionate to the shortening of the payment period) the cash-flow gain still amounted to 133.8 billion euros (5.9 billion euros for the United Kingdom).

There is therefore a very clear increase in liquidity. The Southern European countries would reap the greatest benefits from a reduction of the payment period. This is logical, since they currently have the longest payment periods. A reduction to 30 days would give a huge boost to the liquidity levels of companies in these countries, providing them with cash for much needed reinvestment. The situation is reversed in Northern Europe, where most countries already have good payment discipline. The United Kingdom is in a position somewhere between these two blocks, and will therefore also benefit to some extent from the new payment regulations.

Having said this, the simulation was a relatively simple exercise, which did not take account of many other possibly relevant factors, such as potential loss of turnover, contract negotiation costs, the financial consequences of reduced trade credit, etc.

ATTENTION!

It is open to question whether or not the cultural identity of the Southern European countries can be changed as quickly as the EU seems to think, and that payment terms will really contract so strongly.

3 Official insolvencies (administration, company voluntary arrangements, liquidation)

When we speak of official failures or insolvencies, in the United Kingdom we usually think of administration, company voluntary arrangement (CVA) and liquidation. For the credit insurer, the administration and CVA procedures are equivalent to a liquidation. This may seem like a strange assertion, since the intention of both the administration and the CVA is to give companies a last chance by offering them temporary protection against their creditors. But it is precisely this fact that means that the supplier of the goods and services, and after him the credit insurer, will be forced as part of the final rescue plan to remit part – and perhaps a large part – of the debt owing to them. Consequently, the insurer will be required to pay compensation. Having said this, the insurer will continue to view the matter pragmatically: if the administration or CVA procedure is successful, the company will eventually acquire new credit limits, if its creditworthiness permits.

ATTENTION!

As with payment behaviour, there are significant cultural differences with regard to insolvency (or bankruptcy) in Europe.

3.1 MAJOR DIFFERENCES AT INTERNATIONAL LEVEL

A weak economic cycle, resulting in worse payment behaviour, leads to an increase in the number of official insolvencies. Surveys of failed companies have shown that the payment behaviour of customers (and, in the worst case, the non-payment of outstanding invoices) led to liquidity problems and even

TABLE 2.4 *Official insolvencies: number and annual percentage change (source: Euler Hermes)*

	2009		2010		2011	
	Number	%	Number	%	Number	%
UK	**35,185**	**17**	**29,111**	**- 17**	**30,751**	**6**
USA	60,837	40	56,282	- 7	47,806	- 15
Japan	15,480	- 1	13,321	- 14	12,734	- 4
Germany	32,687	12	31,998	- 2	30,099	- 6
France	64,533	12	63,337	- 2	60,655	- 4
Italy	9,400	29	11,400	21	12,094	6
Spain	5,096	76	4,951	- 3	5,910	19
Netherlands	8,040	73	7,211	- 10	7,140	- 1
Belgium (*)	9,421	11	9,579	2	10,224	7
Poland	673	57	691	3	740	7
China	4,448	- 2	3,715	-16	3,043	- 18

(*) For Belgium the figures reflect bankruptcies only, not WCO procedures (similar to the administration/CVA procedures)

insolvency in 64% of cases. Dealing with this insolvency is the core activity of the credit insurers: they provide cover against the insolvency risk.

When assessing table 2.4, it is important not to pay too much attention to the figures: as a result of differences in national legislation, some countries have almost no bankruptcies, whereas others have considerably more. The parameters are also important: do the figures refer exclusively to companies, or are sole traders and perhaps even private individuals included? The credit insurer only provides cover for the (official) insolvencies of companies and sole traders. Spain has very few bankruptcies, since the associated legal procedures are seldom brought to a final conclusion: they are simply too long and too expensive.

TABLE 2.5 *Insolvency index per country: index 100 = 2000 (source: Euler Hermes)*

	Weight in %	2007	2008	2009	2010	2011
World index	100.0	84	106	133	125	119
UK	**4.3**	**85**	**112**	**131**	**108**	**114**
USA (*)	26.8	80	123	172	159	135
Japan	10.4	75	83	82	71	68
Germany	6.3	103	104	116	113	107
France	4.9	115	133	149	146	140
Italy	3.9	53	62	81	98	104
Spain	2.6	125	350	615	598	714
Netherlands	1.5	129	130	225	201	199
Belgium	0.9	113	125	139	141	151
Poland	0.9	37	33	52	54	57
China	12.9	60	63	62	51	42

(*) A weighting of 26.8% is applied for the USA, whereas this country is only responsible for 22.5% of the world's GDP. The reason is that when the index was being calculated, a number of countries were omitted, so that the relative share of the USA in the index increased. This is also the case – but to a lesser degree – for other countries.

In other words, there are relatively few bankruptcies *de iure*, but *de facto* there are just as many (if not more) as anywhere else. France is an example of a country that takes matters to the opposite extreme.

3.2 THE WORLD INSOLVENCY INDEX

In response to the wide-ranging differences in the official national insolvency statistics, the Euler Hermes credit insurance group developed its own insolvency index. The total nominal number of official insolvencies worldwide (bankruptcies/liquidations, compositions, administrations/CVAs, and other similar procedures in other countries) was deemed to be equivalent to 100 (for indexation) in a given year (2000), so that the evolution of official insolvencies could be monitored year by year. This world insolvency index (see table 2.5 and figure 2.2) is compiled by giving each country a weighting on the basis of its share in global world production. In this way, the emphasis is placed on relative fluctuations, which is more relevant for credit insurers.

In time, this index will be permanently above the 100 level, since the growth of the economy means that the number of companies will continue to increase. Running parallel with this development, the nominal number of official insolvencies will also increase equivalently over time.

FIGURE 2.2 *World insolvency index: index 100 = 2000 (*) (source: national statistics; Euler Hermes)*

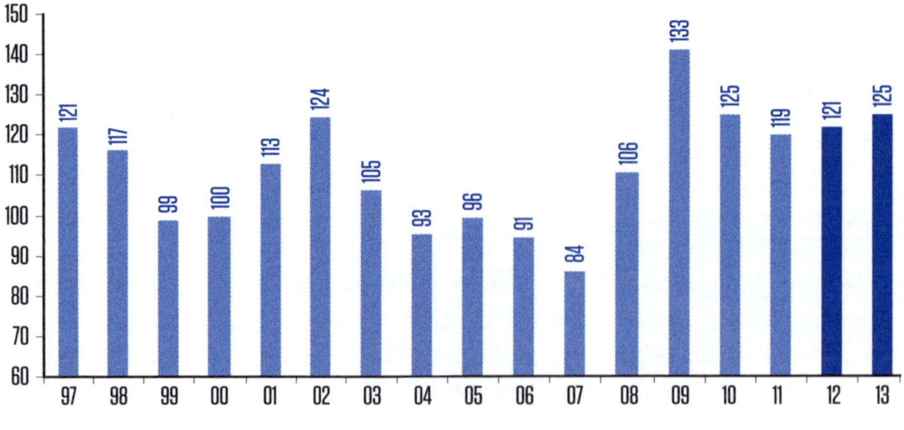

(*) Countries weighted with 2011 GDP at current exchange rates

TABLE 2.6 *Insolvency rates per country in 2009 (source: Euler Hermes)*

	Insolvency rate %	Total no.	Source	Total of companies
USA	1.1	60,837	Adm. Office of US Courts	5,752,975
Japan	1.0	15,480	Tokyo Shoko Research (TSR)	1,515,835
Germany	0.9	32,687	DeStatis	3,551,240
France	2.2	64,533	Euler Hermes SFAC	2,925,124
Italy	0.2	9,400	ISTAT, Movimpresse	4,500,000
Spain	0.2	5,096	Inst. Nacional de Estatistica(INE)	3,355,830
Netherlands	1.0	8,040	CBS	844,450
Belgium	1.2	9,421	NIS	763,831
UK	**1.7**	**35,185**	**The Insolvency Service**	**2,119,660**
Poland	0.0	673	Ministerie van Justitie	3,742,673
China	0.1	4,448	China Court/ Sinotrust's creditlink	4,613,000

In this context, there is probably a better way to calculate the insolvency rate per country in the future: namely the total number of official insolvencies offset against the total number of companies. This would allow the level of risk in each local economy to be more easily monitored. The problem with this method, however, is that it is often difficult to get accurate figures for the total number of companies. We might know for one given year the number of new starters in a country and also have available the relevant official insolvency figures, but there is an unknown number of companies that have simply ceased trading, been dissolved or gone into receivership. These, too, need to be taken into account. The VAT Administration can provide figures about VAT numbers that have been decommissioned, but this information is often provided after a considerable delay and there is no guarantee that the details are complete.

The figures for China and Poland in table 2.6 must be treated with caution. Local statistical techniques in some parts of Asia and Eastern Europe are not as advanced as in, say, Western Europe.

4 Economic turbulence

The administration and CVA procedures aim to offer companies in trouble a second chance by granting them (temporary) protection from the claims of their creditors. On the one hand, it is certainly worthwhile to give companies a second chance to turn things around. On the other hand, it is important that we do not keep structurally weak companies artificially in existence. We are living in a rapidly changing world, where industries come and go (consider the collapse of the mining industry in the United Kingdom during the 1970s and 1980s). This coming and going of companies and sectors is referred to as 'turbulence' in the economy: old, weak enterprises make way for new, stronger ones. In this respect, the net increase in the number of (new) companies, together with the creation rate against the total number of existing companies, can be regarded as an indication of this turbulence. Turbulence creates a new dynamic within the business world, driven by a constant search for innovation and improved methods of production. Strong turbulence leads to a higher level of competition and greater economic growth.

The importance of the life-and-death cycle for the efficient working of an economy cannot be emphasised enough. The economy needs a revolving door. With a sufficient inflow of new companies, but also with an outflow of older companies that gradually disappear. After a number of years, an increase in the number of stoppers is translated into an increase in the number of starters. This is known as 'replacement creativity'. The famous Austrian economist Joseph Schumpeter even talks of 'creative destruction'.

WHAT YOU NEED TO KNOW

Credit insurance plays an important role with regard to economic turbulence. The most important task of credit insurance is a preventative one: a credit insurer will not take risks on companies that may become insolvent in the short term (i.e., less than a year). In this way, the knowledge and expertise that the insurer has acquired over the years is shared with the insured parties. After all, it flies in the face of logic that suppliers should continue to provide goods and services to customer companies that they know have a good chance of 'going under' in the near future. Turnover is only realised when the invoices are actually paid!

In the first instance, the insured supplier is not happy, since he will lose turnover and profits. On the other hand, it forces him to go in search of new prospects with whom he can establish a healthier commercial relationship for the future. In this manner, the business dynamic of the company is maintained. The credit insurer can help the insured party in this search: the insurer has at his disposal a detailed database, with information about thousands and thousands of companies worldwide. Every company has its own rating. This rating is a measure of its solvency as a debtor, based on a number of criteria, focussed specifically on the company's ability to repay what it owes within a period of one year. This rating instrument allows the supplier to identify quickly and easily the companies on which he should target his efforts and acquisitions.

CHAPTER 3
CREDIT MANAGEMENT

In this chapter, we will look at how credit management works in a company. We will then briefly discuss the tools at the disposal of a company to help it guard against insolvency.

1 Good internal credit management

As the global economy and trade relationships have developed, credit management has almost become a subject in itself, rather than remaining a small part (for instance, just credit control) of wider risk-management programmes.

The professional literature on credit management is not extensive. It is still a relatively young discipline – but one which is gradually showing its worth. Since the financial and economic crisis of 2008-2009 in particular, the need for good credit management has received considerable attention. A much wider community than ever before began to realise that outstanding trade accounts can consume huge amounts of a company's hard-earned cash reserves. A great deal of corporate illiquidity stemmed from this and the adage of 'cash is king' accentuated the problem for the trading community. Coupled with the widespread reduction of credit facilities by the banks, companies sought to increase their capital reserves.

The efficient organisation of credit management within a company is a fundamental necessity, if the non-payment of invoices is to be avoided. Here (and again later in the book), we will examine how and why credit management must be an essential element of any meaningful business strategy. As we shall describe later, a company may feel it is more efficient to outsource some elements of its credit management operation. Essentially, however, there has to be a clear management understanding of and control over a company's credit activity, even where parts of it are outsourced.

Finally, we will address the key performance indicators associated with credit management, such as the number of days of customer credit, the days of sales outstanding, and the ageing debtors analysis.

1.1 DEFINITION

Credit management is the monitoring and management of credit that companies extend to their customers in respect of the sale of goods and services. It should exercise control over sales policy in order to ensure that, before any credit term is extended under the contract, the customer has passed a full check on his creditworthiness, and that terms of payment are fully in accordance with corporate policy and cash flow requirements. The supplier grants the customer a given number of days in which to pay the invoice. In other words, he agrees to the temporary postponement of payment. Until this payment is made the supplier has an 'account-receivable' in his bookkeeping. The customer is therefore his debtor. There should be a clear policy in place for credit control, both for monitoring the payment performance of all debtors and for actioning a predetermined set of chasing and recovery plans when payments are overdue.

MISUNDERSTANDING

Credit management has nothing to do with the management of short-term or long-term bank credits, company-issued bonds on the capital market, mortgage credits, etc.

Granting credit means taking on a trade credit risk. Credit management therefore is synonymous with trade debt management. It is a combination of preventative and remedial actions (for example, legal proceedings) that attempt to reduce the risks of, and otherwise deal with, customer default. The objective is to increase the profitability of the company, without harming or ignoring important commercial opportunities.

Credit management therefore implies:

- optimising business transactions and the flow of trade;
- improving the turnover time and circulation of debt capital;
- limiting and managing default risks;
- making a positive contribution towards turnover objectives;
- making a positive contribution towards the economic value of the organisation.

Nevertheless, in many organisations credit management is still seriously undervalued. It is still essentially regarded as an administrative task rather than a matter of policy. For many companies (and for SMEs in particular), the creation of a strong credit management system is not seen as a matter of priority. The monitoring of outstanding accounts receivable is carried out by non-specialist staff, along with their other tasks – if or when they have time.

In most companies credit management usually falls under the responsibility of the company's finance department. The reporting line is usually credit controller to credit manager to the chief financial officer (CFO).

1.2 CREDIT MANAGEMENT AS PART OF THE COMPANY'S RISK MANAGEMENT PROCEDURES

Credit management and the management of outstanding trade accounts is therefore part of the company's risk management procedures. Risk is inherent in the process of 'doing business'. Within a risk management framework, we can see the risk as:

- a future event, the consequences of which are currently unknown but which may become evident in due course;
- a future event which may or may not happen;
- a future event which may or may not cause damage to the company.

Risks can be many and varied: changes in rates of exchange, changes in market conditions, changes in product trends, changes in competitive behaviour, changes in the economic cycle, political risks, technological developments, insolvent customers, fire, natural disaster, etc.

The aim of risk management is to identify the risks to which the company is subject and to minimise the economic and financial consequences of these risks. Viewed in this light, credit management forms an integral part of the general management systems and strategy of a company, with the specific purpose of contributing towards the optimisation of results and long-term business survival.

How to handle these risks is dependent upon the individual circumstances of a company. Credit terms, with their resultant impact on cash-flow, might be handled within its own financial resources and/or existing levels of bank borrowing; or else invoices might be separately financed by such means as factoring or invoice discounting with a third party organisation. The credit risk itself might be considered manageable within the company's own procedures; or perhaps credit insurance can be purchased in order to transfer the indemnified percentage of the risk attached to all outstanding amounts owed by buyers.

1.3 THE DEVELOPMENT OF A CREDIT MANAGEMENT STRATEGY WITHIN A COMPANY

The company's strategy must begin with an analysis of its environment. Michael Porter (the Bishop William Lawrence University Professor at Harvard Business School and a leading authority on company strategy and the competitiveness of nations and regions) has attempted to map the external environment of a company and transform it into a specific and effective strategy. He did this on the basis of five competitive elements, which have a dominant influence on the profitability of a market. These elements are depicted in figure 3.1. Three of these elements have a direct impact on a company's competitive position. Who are our current competitors? Who are the new actors in the market and what threat do they present? Are there alternative products? The other two elements are the customers and the suppliers: two of the company's most important stakeholders. Porter later added a sixth external stakeholder: the government.

FIGURE 3.1 *Environment analysis for strategy development (source: Michael Porter, Competitive Strategy)*

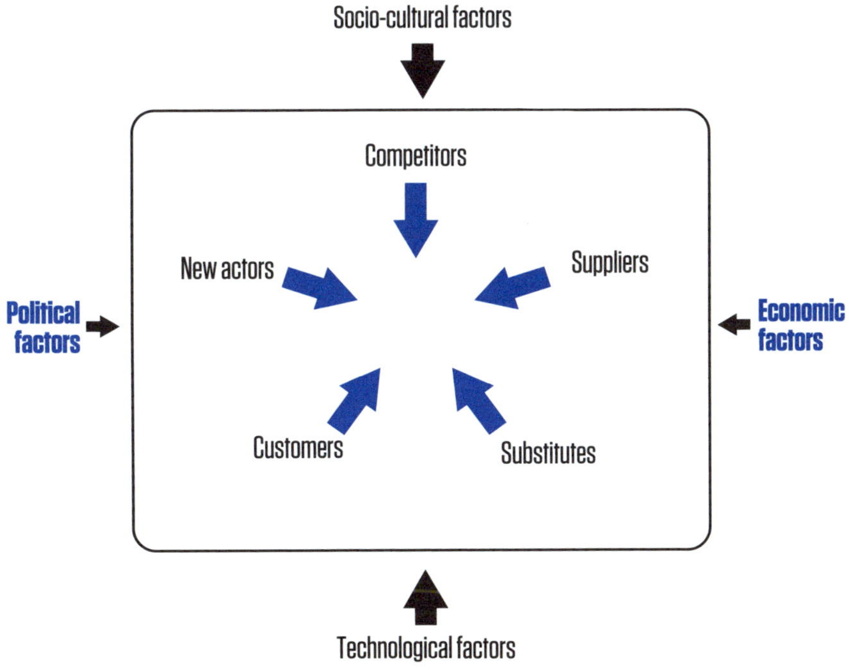

FOOD FOR THOUGHT

When we talk about customers and suppliers, we are usually thinking first and foremost about the purely commercial aspects of doing business. But they are also stakeholders, who are closely involved in the processes of credit insurance.

Before we can speak of good credit management within a company, it is important that the financial and commercial departments are on the same wavelength. At first glance, they seem to have contradictory interests:

- the finance department wants the lowest possible number of unpaid bills;
- the commercial department wants the highest possible level of turnover.

Good communication between these departments is necessary, in order to prevent them from each becoming locked in their own ivory tower, which can only do harm to the company. This means that the company's general objectives must be defined in the light of a requirement for good credit management. In this context, we can conclude that the formula for the global profit of the company should be formulated as follows:

**Maximum volumes of sales + prompt payment +
minimum volume of bad debts**

If sales increase, but at the same time cash-flow is declining because of the late payment or non-payment of invoices, company policy needs to be urgently revised. Or as someone once expressed it: 'Sales are vanity, profit is sanity'. A sale is only a successful sale when the customer has fulfilled his obligations – and paid the bill.

To make this possible, the credit management function must first determine a credit strategy and policy that is appropriate within its company. This requires decisions to be taken on the following three issues:

1. The credit norm or the minimum level of creditworthiness with which the customer/debtor must comply (i.e., how much is the company prepared to let the customer have on credit?). This sets a credit limit. A score or rating from an external third party can be an objective way to determine this matter.

2 The credit conditions: immediate cash payment or payment after a period of time?
3 The debt collection procedures: how will the company react when a customer fails to settle his invoice on time?

Once these issues have been decided, they can be transformed at an organisational level into an effective credit management policy, which may (if desired) make use of outsourcing agencies, such as credit insurers, factoring companies and debt collectors.

On the basis of the chosen risk management policy, credit limits are then set in respect of customers, and a series of credit control procedures are put in place to check whether or not customers are actually settling their debts by the agreed due dates of payment.

The efficiency of the implemented credit management policy (with default monitoring forming a key part of the process) can be measured with reference to a series of key performance indicators (KPIs), such as the number of days of outstanding customer credit and the ageing debts analysis. We will be looking more closely at these matters in section 1.4 of this chapter.

It is important to realise that good credit management has a positive commercial impact: it leads to a better knowledge of customers and the market in which they operate. This knowledge can be further deepened through the development of a customer relationship management (CRM) programme. CRM applies different methods and techniques to assess, steer and optimise relations with customers. Data stored in IT systems in respect of existing (and potential) customers are analysed and used for this purpose.

On the basis of this information, the company can draw up its own debt collection strategy: less satisfactory customers who fail to settle their invoices on time can be dealt with more assertively. This all leads to an important added value, which in turn makes a contribution towards the creation of greater shareholder value.

1.4 SOME KEY PERFORMANCE INDICATORS (KPI'S) FOR CREDIT MANAGEMENT

→ *General*

TABLE 3.1 *Importance of the use (in % terms) of various performance indicators for credit control and debt recovery in Europe (source: Credit Management Research Centre, Leeds University Business School / Euler Hermes 2006)*

	Days sales outstanding (DSO)	Cash recovery targets	Ratio bad debts/sales	Write off of bad debts
All countries	69	36	54	20
Belgium	43	60	27	13
France	81	14	74	29
Germany	47	40	67	33
Netherlands	47	47	50	9
Hungary	41	29	57	25
Italy	54	17	53	20
Spain	75	25	68	8
Poland	73	64	55	27
Portugal	81	32	47	24
UK	**80**	**37**	**51**	**15**

We can see from table 3.1 that DSO (days sales outstanding) is the most popular indicator, particularly in countries such as France, Portugal and the UK. These figures reflect the penetration of credit management in Europe: the countries where DSO is the most frequently used point of reference also in general have a more well-established culture of structured credit management, with a separate credit department as a key part of the company's operations.

The figures show that at that time France, Portugal and the UK were the most advanced countries in this respect.

We will now look in a little more detail at the three most commonly used key performance indicators (KPIs):

1 number of days of customer credit (equivalent to a DSO over 365 days);
2 DSO; and
3 the ageing debts analysis.

These are all indicators that can be used to measure the efficiency of credit management within a company. There are also a number of secondary indicators, such as the amount of bad debts as a proportion of total annual turnover.

→ *Number of days of customer credit*

The longer the duration of the average payment period, the greater the risk of non-payment. It is therefore important for a company to know the average length of time that its customers are taking to pay (as opposed to the credit terms notionally being given). The classic ratio used for this purpose is the total number of days of customer credit in relation to the total annual turnover. The formula is therefore:

$$\frac{\text{accounts receivable within a maximum of 1 year} - \text{any advances received (and booked in)}}{\text{annual turnover (including VAT)}} \times 365$$

The calculation is therefore made on the basis of a full year. If the actual average time for the settlement of accounts receivable is greater than the credit period notionally being given in current contracts and/or set down as one of the parameters in the credit policy, the company will need to initiate measures to improve this situation. Prompt and effective action, with the help of credit insurance, will usually enable the average number of customer credit days to be reduced.

When analysing this ratio, it is also important to:
- → take account of the customary usage in the sector: some sectors have an average payment term that is long, while other sectors are more focussed on shorter periods;
- → take due account of developments over time: if the general trend of average payment time in recent years is downwards, the situation is under control, even if there are occasional upward fluctuations;
- → remember that an unusually low DSO compared to your industry standard may mean you are too cautious with your credit terms, which may, in turn, be inhibiting sales.

It is also necessary to take account of seasonal influences: in some sectors a large portion of the turnover is concentrated in a relatively short period each year (for example, the sale of diaries in December), which can lead to wide variations in the average figures throughout the year.

→ *Days sales outstanding*

The use of the total number of customer credit days as described in the above example is a DSO calculation for the company over an entire year. The DSO can also be calculated for a more limited period of the company's own choosing (most commonly 90 days). Such a DSO calculation will allow the company to track changes in the average payment period over time.

$$\frac{\text{outstanding accounts receivable at the end of the chosen period}}{\text{turnover during the chosen period (e.g. 90 days)}} \times \text{number of days in the chosen period (e.g. 90 days)}$$

Table 3.2 shows the classic way of calculating a DSO for periods of 30, 60 and 90 days. You can see the sales per month and also when the payments in respect of these sales are received in the following months. The starting point for the DSO calculation at the end of the quarter in March is the amount of the remaining outstanding payments (accounts receivable) = 350 (100+200+300-20-70-160). The DSO is then worked out as follows:

- 30 days: the outstanding amount (350) is compared with the sales turnover for the final month (March = 300) and then multiplied by 30.
- 60 days: the outstanding amount (350) is compared with the sales turnover for the last two months (February and March = 500) and then multiplied by 60.
- 90 days: the outstanding amount (350) is compared with the sales turnover for all three months (January, February and March = 600) and then multiplied by 90.

TABLE 3.2 *Calculation of the DSO*

(x thousand euro)		Incoming payments					
	Sales	Jan	Feb	Mar	Apr	May	Jun
Q I (first quarter)							
Jan	100	20	30	40	10		
Feb	200		40	60	80	20	
Mar	300			60	90	120	30
Total receipts per month		*20*	*70*	*160*			
Total outstanding amount at end of month		**80**	**210**	**350**			
DSO-30					35		
DSO-60					42		
DSO-90					52.5		

MISUNDERSTANDING

DSO is important, but it is disappointing to note that discussions within many companies about credit management do not go beyond this point. Credit management is much broader than just DSO (creditworthiness analysis, debt recovery policy, management of working capital, etc.), although it cannot be denied that DSO is an important cornerstone of any credit management policy.

When interpreting DSO, it is important to bear the following points in mind. DSO is the end result of all the factors relating to customer credits: the negotiated payment period, the payment behaviour of the customer, the effectiveness of the debt recovery activities, etc. Moreover, it is also possible that unpaid invoices, which have been outstanding for longer periods (e.g. because of a dispute), can have an exaggerated negative impact on the DSO calculation. Nevertheless, it is useful for a company to have figures relating to the totality of its global credit management policy, even though these figures reflect different functions and different areas of responsibility.

→ *Ageing analysis of accounts receivable*

Outstanding amounts (current accounts receivable, unpaid past due invoices) are classified by age. This age pattern is obtained by calculating the total amount of the outstanding amounts in a particular age category, expressed as a proportion of all the outstanding amounts. Table 3.3 shows how this is done.

USEFUL TIPS

The situation is a cause for concern if the highest percentages are found in the oldest age categories: this significantly increases the likelihood that some of these outstanding amounts will never be settled. It is clear that credit insurance, linked to the effective monitoring of invoices, can produce much better results in the context of an ageing analysis of accounts receivable. If the follow-up of invoices is poor, the insured party may risk having his cover withdrawn by his credit insurer on these invoices. It is worth noting, however, that many credit insurers do provide an in-house collections facility as part of their policy.

TABLE 3.3 *Ageing analysis of accounts receivable*

Age of accounts receivable	Amount (x thousand euro)	% of total outstanding accounts receivable
0-30 days	160	57.14%
31-60 days	100	35.71%
61-90 days	20	7.15%
More than 90 days	0	0%
Total	*280*	*100%*

2 Other tools for combating insolvency

Credit insurance is an instrument that allows companies to protect themselves against the risk of the eventual non-payment of their trade receivables and the possible insolvency of their debtors. But private credit insurance is not the only weapon at their disposal. Several other useful tools are also available.

In 2008, a survey was conducted amongst 1,198 companies in six European countries, in collaboration with the German Financial Times. 65% of the companies questioned said that they took steps to guard against the negative consequences of bad debt. When asked to specify which steps they took, 30% answered that they made use of credit insurance. The other instruments they mentioned included:

- cash payment in advance: 17%;
- active internal debt recovery procedures: 13%;
- external debt recovery service: 11%;
- letters of credit: 6%;
- sureties/guarantees: 4%;
- cash payment on delivery: 3%;
- retention of title: 2%;
- factoring: 1%.

Other possible remedies not mentioned in this list include:

- Collective guarantee funds, such as the ABTA Bond in the UK for the travel sector. These funds are usually made compulsory by law and are frequently initiated to offer protection to members of the public (in particular) against the possible consequences of company insolvencies. There are examples of such funds in both the public and private sectors.
- Suretyship insurance (the policyholder can be the debtor, who pays the premium to a surety company in return for the issue of a bond, guaranteeing his performance); this product is related to credit insurance (where the policyholder is the creditor – see above). It is most common in the construction and building trades.
- Documentary collection.

In other words, credit management within a company can make use of many different tools and procedures.

- Credit insurance is one of the more common external measures: the company can transfer a proportion of its risk to a third party in return for the payment of a premium. This essentially gives the company experienced assistance with its credit management for the totality of its outstanding trade receivables.
- Internal measures allow the company to cover the default risk case by case, if they so wish. In this instance, there is no general approach. The products taken usually involve banking products: documentary credits, documentary collections, etc.

3 The outsourcing of credit management: the credit insurer as global credit manager

GOOD TO KNOW

In one sense, the credit insurer can be described as a global, world-oriented credit manager. Just like a company, he manages a huge portfolio of debtor risks. He supports the supplier, who is his client (insured party), acting almost as a kind of alter ego.

The credit manager is therefore confronted with all the different aspects of credit management, just like companies in their capacity as the suppliers of goods and services. It is therefore only logical that some aspects of credit management in this book are viewed from the perspective of the insurer; for example, retention of title.

PART 2

Operational and technical aspects

In chapter 4 we will discuss the techniques involved in putting together a credit insurance policy. Thereafter in chapter 5 we will look at the manner in which the credit insurer analyses the creditworthiness of a company. Chapter 6 will explore the world of credit ratings.

CHAPTER 4
THE TECHNIQUES OF CREDIT INSURANCE

In this more technical chapter, we will give a summary of the practical elements that make up a typical credit insurance policy. The persons contractually concerned with this policy are the insurer and the insured party (the supplier), but the important position of the debtor should not be overlooked.

The following summary is based on the standard clauses in existing policies and credit insurance marketing literature. We have sought to find common denominators where possible (the schedules we have used come from Euler Hermes). This means that we will not look closely at the specific characteristics of the many different policies on offer, but will focus on their common elements, with the turnover policy as the central theme.

HOW IT IS

In this chapter, you will come across numerous technical terms. Above all, however, it is important that you understand the philosophy behind the technical working of a credit insurance policy. At first sight, this may appear complex, but in reality it is based on a number of simple principles.

1 Credit insurance as a working instrument

We shall see that for the duration of the policy an active collaboration exists between the credit insurer and his insured customer. As we said in our introduction, it is possible, especially for the manufacturer of tailor-made products or those manufacturing to the buyer's specific design requirements, to cover the risk of contracts in hand in the pre-delivery period. We will talk in more detail about this later, but, for the moment, we will confine our comments to the more standard forms of cover that commence on delivery of the goods or services.

WHAT YOU NEED TO KNOW

The method of working described below shows clearly that credit insurance allows plenty of room for freedom of choice in the relationship between the credit insurer and the policyholder. After all, both parties are corporate professionals in their own field, so that it is assumed that they both understand the issues at stake.

1.1 CREDIT DECISIONS

Once the broad terms and conditions of the prospective credit insurance policy are understood, the relationship, which is unique to the two parties, begins at the moment when the insured party asks the insurer to set credit limits for his customers. The decision with regard to these limits is then taken by the insurer.

→ *Applying for credit limits*

The simple act of signing a credit insurance policy does not mean that the insured party automatically has cover for possible default in respect of his outstanding accounts receivable. To obtain this, he must first make a credit limit application to the insurer for the setting of individual customer credit limits. The purpose of these limits is to set the maximum level of risk for which the insured party is covered against each of his debtors. The payment period granted by the insured party to his customers is an important factor in the setting of these limits: the longer the payment period, the greater the potential for late payment or default. The credit application can be made online. In order to speed up the process and avoid any potential misunderstandings, it is crucial that the correct identification of each debtor is given, with full details of name, address and local company registration number.

USEFUL TIP

Always try to give the local company registration number of the debtor. This will allow the application to be processed more quickly. Every country has its own identification code (see appendix 1). If you do not have this number, the other information must be as accurate as possible: name, address, legal form (public company, limited company, etc.). With limits being underwritten in the majority of countries worldwide, accuracy is paramount. The VAT number is used most widely, along with the registration number relative to that market. As credit insurers now have an underwriting presence in many countries, their database of buyers is growing constantly. Many policyholders may have already obtained a status report on their customer and this should also provide the necessary registration and VAT numbers.

In principle, the insured party cannot apply for limits to be set for customers who are already in default. For example, a customer is in default if he has failed to settle his outstanding debt within the agreed maximum extension period (MEP). This is a maximum period specified in the policy agreement to extend the original due date for payment of any debt.

→ *How do you set the credit limit amount?*

With a one-off contract, the figure will be the anticipated maximum amount that will become owing in respect of delivered goods or services.

With a regular and constant monthly turnover figure, the calculation can be made on the basis of the following formula:

Requested limit = A x (B+1), where
A = annual turnover / 12
B = actual period of payment expressed in months

> EXAMPLE
> **Monthly turnover = 1,000,000 euro**
> **Payment period = 60 days**
> **This means that the insured party needs to ask for a credit limit of at least € 1,000,000 euros x (2+1) = 3,000,000 euros.**

Another alternative is to use the highest monthly turnover figure, multiplied by the actual payment period expressed in months.

Where the turnover of the insured party is subject to seasonal or other fluctuations, it will be necessary to ensure that the highest levels of outstandings are covered. (It should be borne in mind that VAT is not normally covered, so if this is included in the outstandings figure, the limit requirement will be proportionally less.) The credit insurer will always try to accommodate seasonal requirements, but in some circumstances he may wish to monitor the actual usage or uptake of the higher figure. (One example might be where there is very high demand for cover on a particular buyer from a wide range of insured customers or where there is information highlighting difficulties in the trade sector or even with the particular buyer.) It is quite common, in these circumstances, for underwriters to issue only temporary limits.

Later, we shall see that in reality the levels of cover agreed by the credit insurer are often much higher than the insured party really needs.

→ *The credit decision*

The credit insurer can react to the credit application in one of three ways:

1 Acceptance: the insurer has full confidence in the situation and sets a limit.
2 Partial acceptance: the insurer has a degree of confidence, but there are still doubts about the debtor's ability to repay the sums that will become owed on time; the insurer may also conclude that the requested credit limit is too high or does not reflect the reality of the situation (for example, based on the turnover or suppliers' credit in the annual account of the debtor).
3 Refusal: the insurer does not trust the creditworthiness of the debtor (e.g. because he is in receipt of adverse information about poor business figures, the number of unpaid invoices outstanding, etc.). NB: Recent experience suggests that more and more companies are filing their returns with the relevant authorities late, in order to hide their deteriorating performance for as long as possible.

The final decision taken by the underwriting department of the credit insurer is as much an art as an exact science: experience and knowledge of the trade sector in question have been developed from a wide spectrum of information sources, including other insured parties. As a result, discussions are often held with the buyer in question, as well as other relevant parties.

In cases of refusal and partial acceptance, the insured party will not always be happy, since the turnover that he wishes to achieve with his customer is not fully covered against possible default. It will always be open for him to appeal against such a decision. Especially if he feels that he is in possession of information that the underwriter does not (yet) have at his disposal. Of course, he is still free to do more business with the customer than the limit allows, but he does so at his own risk in respect of any loss in excess of the agreed limit (if there is one). Also, it should be borne in mind that the premium is payable on turnover, not on the credit limit. Nevertheless, it should not be overlooked that the added value of credit insurance in these circumstances is that the insured party now knows that his customer is not 100% creditworthy and that consequently it would be unwise to allow him too much latitude with regard to the settlement of his invoices. Forewarned is forearmed. This is risk prevention at work.

When taking his credit decision, the insurer is free to impose certain conditions, such as the setting of a new maximum payment period, the provision of quarterly business figures, etc. Sometimes a personal guarantee is demanded but this is the exception, not the rule.

MISUNDERSTANDING

It is often said that credit insurers only insure 'good' customers. This is not the case. The fact that the insurer bases his premium exclusively on the insurable turnover encourages him to support as far as possible the customer's credit limit applications. This means taking 'responsible' risks, based on a sound knowledge of clients and customers. Yet even with 'responsible' risks, economic swings, trade sector fluctuations and the vagaries of human management failings will always ensure that payment defaults arise from time to time. On average, in simple terms, the difference between income on the one hand and costs plus claims paid on the other hand determines the resultant profit or loss for the credit insurer. With increasing costs necessitated by investment in skilled people, the gathering of information and the installation of IT systems, credit insurers will clearly aim to pay out less than the collected premiums in any one year. The insurers fixed costs usually amount to 30% of his premium receipts. However, whilst it is correct to say that credit insurers have had some excellent years in the past, with loss ratios being as low as 35-40%, in other years the results have been much less satisfactory. In 2008-09, for example, loss ratios for some credit insurers were well over 100%.

In principle, payment terms depend on the type of goods/ services involved. In general, if consumer goods are involved, the supplier wants to receive payment before those goods are consumed (usually monthly account terms or up to 60 days at most). For others, more permanently identifiable goods, capital goods and larger items of equipment manufactured by the supplier, the payment period can be longer, but special policies are usually designed to cope with such exceptions. Standard policies have maximum terms of 180 days, including the maximum extension period (MEP).

MISUNDERSTANDING

Another much-heard misconception is that credit insurers frequently work with maximum ceilings. This has been taken to mean that the combined limits on a debtor may not exceed a certain maximum level of risk and that new credit applications that take the exposure of that debtor over this level will be treated unfavourably. In exceptional cases of very large commercial risks, this can indeed occur and the overall capacity to take on risk is limited by an insurer's own capital strength. However (as we will describe later), this capacity can be enhanced considerably by the purchase of reinsurance.

The reality, therefore, is that for the vast majority of cases all insured parties are treated the same and in general, reinsurance capacity is sufficient to meet market requirements.

Limit decisions are generally notified by email or via on-line systems (e.g. Euler Hermes has their EOLIS system). Every decision is also coded with its own unique number for ease of identification. Such decision notifications can either be a direct response to the insured party's credit application, or can be issued at the initiative of the insurer if, for example, the credit status of a debtor deteriorates (within the framework of the monitoring process). The policyholder can save on limit and monitoring fees (unless he is on a fixed limits fee policy) by relinquishing non-required credit limits. This is looked on very favourably by underwriters, since it not only releases unused risk, but also provides a true reflection of the risk they are insuring.

→ *Excluded debtors*

Because of the level or nature of their risk, some debtors are automatically refused a credit limit. These are the so-called 'excluded' debtors, and include:

- → Private individuals. The credit insurance covered in this book is essentially a business-to-business (B2B) product. A private individual does not have a company registration number.
- → Companies that are in some way or other closely associated with the supplier (insured party). Effectively, this means where there is a shareholding of more than 20% in another entity or any representation on the board of directors of the company in question. The reason for this exclusion is that the insured party would be able to exercise influence on the insolvency risk of the debtor, so that a conflict of interests may arise. As a result, it is assumed that the insured party does not need 'protection' from such associated companies: he is fully familiar with the situation and should have confidence in the people who are effectively his partners.
- → Government organisations. Private credit insurers do not offer insolvency/ default cover for contracts with governmental bodies in the OECD countries (the state, provinces, local authorities, state-controlled agencies, etc.). These bodies cannot be declared insolvent and therefore form no credit risk. (Nevertheless, private credit insurers are increasingly offering cover for short-term political risks. We will look at this in more detail later, but for the moment it is simply enough to note that any default by a government, municipal or state entity would be considered as a political cause of loss, rather than a commercial one.)

The following matters are also excluded from the policy (and are therefore not included in the calculation of the premium):

- → Turnover that is paid in cash or for which the risk is limited or removed through the use of some other financial instrument (for example, bank guarantees). Payment by cheque on delivery is not considered to be a cash payment, since there is a clear credit risk if there are insufficient funds in the bank account of the debtor to cover the cheque. Consequently, this method of payment is generally included.
- → Non-solvent debtors for whom the insurer does not grant a credit line.
- → Commercial transactions that are illegal or constitute a breach of public order (for example, drugs trafficking).

→ *Confidentiality*

Traditionally, credit insurers have contractually insisted on confidentiality in their policies. In the past, they took the view that the insurance was only a matter of concern for the two parties entering into the contract. They therefore retained the right to cancel the policy if this condition was breached, in the event that such a breach, in itself, was likely to cause loss.

However, in more recent times, as credit insurance has increased its penetration of the market-place, it has become customary for a more considered stance to be taken. These restrictive conditions no longer exist in most credit insurance policies, but circumstances can arise in which credit insurers are asked to sign confidentiality agreements with both the policyholders and the insured buyers. The financial crisis of 2008-09 was a catalyst in this respect. The media was full of stories about credit insurance cover having been withdrawn from buyers. As the number of limits on companies in trouble was reduced or further cover became unavailable, the buyers in question simply assumed, based on their knowledge of the market-place, that a lack of credit insurance cover was to blame. Governments opened a dialogue with the credit insurers with a view to offering some form of top-up cover in certain cases. This idea did not really get very far, before greater stability eventually returned to the market. However, it is now fairly common practice for credit analysts from the credit insurers to visit buyers to talk through and/or receive financial information that will help them in their decision-making. The insured parties themselves often set up such meetings, by introducing the credit insurer to the buyer.

ATTENTION!

Sometimes, it may still be necessary for credit insurers to sign confidentiality agreements with both policyholders and insured buyers.

1.2 MONITORING

Monitoring the risk is a hugely important aspect of the credit insurer's work. After the underwriter has made his initial credit decision, it is vital to check regularly whether or not the creditworthiness of the debtor in question remains good. This risk-control process (or monitoring) involves the regular review of underwriting exposure. Priority is given to buyer-exposures where the initial internal rating assessment no longer appears to justify the current levels of exposure. With poor ratings, the level of exposure will be lower. With high ratings, only the cases with a high level of exposure will be monitored. The ratings themselves are reviewed throughout the year with regular reviews in response to annual filed accounts.

To carry out this task, the credit insurer has at his disposal an extensive database, which is regularly updated with both internal and external information, such as payment performance information from all policyholders, monthly management information, purchase ledger and order book discussions, etc. All the risk files can be programmed to give warning signals.

→ *Warning signals for unpaid debts*

An underwriter is obliged to notify a policyholder of adverse information if it impacts on the credit limits he is offering. The downgrading of a buyer, however, may nonetheless mean that he is still financially able to settle his debts. If the underwriters have private and confidential information, they cannot share the details of this information with the policyholder. They can, however, advise him that they have adverse information and that he should trade with caution, if at all.

> **ATTENTION!**
>
> A debtor with liquidity problems will first try to secure a further deferment of payment from the supplier, who has sometimes had a long personal and commercial relationship with the debtor in question.

Within the framework of the policy, the policyholder is also obliged to inform the credit insurer when the payment of an invoice is more than x days overdue (MEP) in relation to its original payment date. Obviously, the correct identification of the debtor is of crucial importance in such cases. The insured party has two options:

- If he is inclined to agree with a specific request from the buyer, he can ask the insurer for an extension of the payment period. The credit insurer needs to agree to any extension beyond the maximum extension period (MEP). Any payment plan to arrange for payment before MEP expiry does not need to involve the insurer.

→ If there has been no satisfactory response to his attempts to recover the monies due or if his request for an extension has been rejected, he must pass the case for third party collection. Each policy has a protracted default period (see below) for collection action to be undertaken; if the debt is still outstanding after this period a claim is payable. It is worth stating that a claim can be assessed whilst any collection action is being made to speed up the claims process should the debt not be settled promptly.

The use of extensions may help to avoid the potential negative spiral that can eventually lead to insolvency. In this way, the insured party can continue to deliver to the debtor; and the debtor, who is experiencing temporary funding difficulties, can continue to generate turnover of his own and so maintain his capacity to repay what he owes. Depending on the scale of the problem, the credit insurer might well wish to meet with the debtor directly, in order to get to the root of the problem. The decision to continue supporting credit terms or the extension of payment may depend on the attitude of the banks or other debenture-holders, as well as the trading performance and future viability of the buyer. It is important that the credit insurer is aware of the general situation and continues to monitor its progress, so that he can initiate other measures if the situation worsens. With this in mind, some underwriters require disputed items to be reported. Whilst these items are not insured, the collation of such information is important, since it paints an overall picture of the buyer's debt and his ability to settle them.

The notification of unpaid accounts receivable to the insurer usually takes place 60 days from the original due date for payment. This is commonly known as the maximum extension period (MEP). Any goods despatched and or services provided to the insured buyer are not covered once the MEP has expired.

There is however a period of grace (usually 14 days) to formally report an overdue account to the insurer at which point the case will usually be passed for collection by a third party agency. The 14 day period of grace is to notify the insurer of a debt outstanding beyond the MEP and to either instruct collection action by the insurers preferred route or to state that action is being taken elsewhere. This period starts at the same time as does the protracted default period. If the insured party neglects to report his overdue, he might loose his right for compensation.

Experience shows that more than 80% of unpaid invoices are settled within a month of the expiry of the payment date. Some debtors pay systematically late if there is no sanction to persuade them to do otherwise.

For reasons of efficiency, it is also logical that some credit insurers only wish to be informed of serious cases of default (beyond the MEP), and not of cases where it is initially a question of payment being disputed (for example, because goods were faulty). This default information is the really crucial information. As a result of the growth of the credit insurance sector at international level, the payment and default experiences of all the insured parties throughout the world who insure with the same credit insurance group quickly become common knowledge among its underwriters.

If the insurer is provided with negative information and if the situation is considered to be a serious one, he will almost certainly act restrictively. To begin with, he might revoke or reduce the credit limit that he has previously granted. This sends a signal to the insured party, who now knows that he must be careful and must not give his customer too much further leeway with regard to the continued postponement of payment. It also provides the trigger for consultation to take place between the relevant parties with regard to the specific circumstances of the case and a remedial plan of action. Once a debt has reached its MEP and has been reported to the insurer, any future deliveries to the buyer must be agreed by the underwriter and a salvage waiver will be required. Otherwise, all monies received (even for advance deliveries) will be allocated chronologically against the oldest outstanding debt.

It sometimes happens that a termination or serious reduction of an existing limit will be postponed or suspended by the credit insurer, despite the deteriorating situation of the insured party's customer. He may consider the full termination of all existing limits to be too drastic an option, which could only make the funding position of the debtor that much worse. If this were to happen, it is likely that all the other interested parties would start to put pressure on the customer; for example, by demanding immediate cash payment for any new deliveries. However, at the same time it is also perfectly feasible that the credit insurer will decide not to accept any further applications for new credit limits on that particular customer. As we have already seen, recent events following the crash of the financial markets in 2008 revealed only too clearly that general awareness of a strong restrictive approach on the part of the insurer can quickly spread through the market, so that even non-insured suppliers begin to demand cash payment from the beleaguered debtor. This points to the need for greater dialogue between insurers, insured customers and buyers.

MISUNDERSTANDING

The perception that the credit insurer is likely to back out of the risk at the first sign of trouble is false. The credit insurer must be careful to ensure that the rapid withdrawal of credit limits does not exacerbate the position, since this would result in precisely the loss (and the need to pay compensation) that he is seeking to avoid. This is why the first restrictive step is usually an investigation of the real use of the limits with the insured party (known as a buyer review), followed by a fully updated investigation into the buyer's financial position and his likely ability to overcome his cash-flow problems. Once this has been established, confidence can be rebuilt and all existing limits can be adjusted to reflect the new situation.

GOOD TO KNOW

Credit insurance therefore implies a continuing and active credit management contribution on the part of the insured party throughout the duration of the policy. As a result, credit insurance is a valuable day-to-day working tool and management instrument. In this sense, it is very different from most other forms of insurance. It is not an insurance that only interests you on renewal or when a claim needs to be made.

→ *Start and finish of the cover provided by an agreed credit limit*

In order to be valid, the credit insurance policy must be active and the premiums due must have been paid. The agreed credit limit will be either a discretionary limit justified under the terms of the policy or a credit limit specifically granted by the underwriter on a named buyer. In general, this credit limit is a permanent limit, applicable to all the invoices issued during the duration period of the policy. In many cases, the limit is backdated to the start of the current policy period rather than the date of the application. If a zero limit has previously been in place, the new positive decision will not be retrospective. If there has been a change in the level of cover previously granted, the insured supplier should seek clarification with regard to the effective starting date.

Renewal of the policy means that all permanent limits are automatically carried over. The only exception is where the underwriter has issued a 'temporary limit', which will have a specific date of expiry. Liability will attach to all undisputed debt owing in respect of delivered goods and services, up to the total value of the agreed credit limit.

GOOD TO KNOW

One of the typical features of a credit insurance policy is its 'revolving' nature. It is possible that the credit limit has already been reached when a new delivery of goods is made. However, as soon as payment for an earlier delivery is settled (either partially or in full) by the buyer, new margin is created within the credit limit and can be used in respect of new deliveries. This means that the limit is revolving for as long as it remains in force (and is not reduced or terminated).

Cover for further deliveries ends when a credit limit is terminated or withdrawn, or when the underlying policy is not renewed, or when a temporary limit has reached its expiry date. Nevertheless, risks in respect of all deliveries which were made before the validity of the credit limit expired, will continue to enjoy full cover under the conditions of the policy. Credit insurers provide 'delayed effect' cover at point of limit cancellation for most customers. This is a maximum period of 30 days, during which the policyholder can continue to deliver orders. In high-risk cases the underwriter may reduce this delayed effect period to just a few days. Most policies include a set period for non-cancellable contract cover, which can be for a period of 3 – 6 months, depending on the policy type. In the event of a claim, the onus is on the policyholder to prove that the contracts he fulfilled with the buyers were legally binding.

Most policies also foresee that cover will not attach to deliveries that are made after the buyer has remained overdue in respect of earlier deliveries for longer than the agreed extension period, as detailed in the policy terms (usually the 60 days of the MEP).

1.3 COLLECTION PROCEDURES

When a compensation claim is made, the principle sum of the claim should cover all the unpaid date-expired and non-expired invoices outstanding against the debtor. The claim must be submitted to the insurer with all necessary supporting documents.

> **HOW TO AVOID PROBLEMS**
>
> When a debtor defaults on payment, the insured party must notify the insurer. This must be done within the timeframe specified in the policy: if the insured party waits too long, he may lose his right to compensation. The philosophy behind this reasoning is that the insurer risks losing everything (to other creditors) if remedial action against the debtor is unduly delayed. The quicker the reaction, the greater the chance of recovery (partial or full) of the outstanding sums.

We can speak of default or impending loss if:

- the debtor has still not paid after the expiry of any extended payment period;
- the debtor has filed for insolvency (administration, company voluntary arrangement (CVA), liquidation, or some other similar legal settlement);
- seizure measures have been instigated against the debtor;
- a bill of exchange/dishonoured cheque protest has been submitted against the debtor;
- in contracts for the issue of goods against acceptance of a bill of exchange, the debtor has not taken up the goods or documents within 60 days of the date of first presentation;
- loss has occurred through a political or other equivalent risk.

The insured party must take all reasonable measures to avoid loss. The collection or recovery can take one of three forms.

1. At the initiative of the insured customer. If he takes this step (for example, through the dispatch of formal letters of reminder), the insurer will lend him all necessary assistance and will follow up the matter closely. The insured party can also make use of an external collection service, specialised in debt recovery. If he chooses to follow his own path of recovery action, the insured party must keep the insurer fully informed of all developments.

2 Any proposals for a phased repayment plan must first be agreed with the insurer.
3 Most of the major credit insurance companies now have a financial shareholding in their own collection operations, so that recovery action can be facilitated easily. For example, customers insured by Euler Hermes are automatically opted in to their collections company and they sign the debt over to them at the point of reporting. Full or partial opt-outs are available, if required.

In some cases, depending on the type of policy, the insured party can (or must) request that the insurer attempts directly to secure settlement of the unpaid invoices. Most insurers have dedicated departments specialised in claims recovery, either by mutual agreement or through due process of law. Having said this, legal proceedings are generally best avoided, if at all possible: they are expensive, time-consuming and demanding.

It is, above all, in cases of protracted default (suspected insolvency) that the collection procedure takes on a more dynamic form. In cases of official insolvency, the insurer's contribution will be limited to:

- the notification of a claim on the liabilities of the insolvent debtor;
- obtaining confirmation of the validity of this claim (in general, from the official receiver or liquidator);
- the follow-up of the dividend payments to the creditors-suppliers;
- the realisation of any guarantees (the liquidation of joint surety bonds, the application of retention of title clauses, etc.).

ATTENTION!

It is important to be aware of the distinction between claims and collections. Claims are made against the credit insurer by its insured customers. Collections are received from the buyers of goods and services, following an earlier instance of non-payment. Specialist collections companies operate independently and not necessarily – or exclusively – on behalf of insured companies.

According to figure 4.1, you first have the maximum extension period (MEP), the end of which is the startpoint of the protracted default period. This protracted default period is in the UK standard 90 days, (but usually brought forward

FIGURE 4.1 *Schedule and timeline for a claim (source: Euler Hermes)*

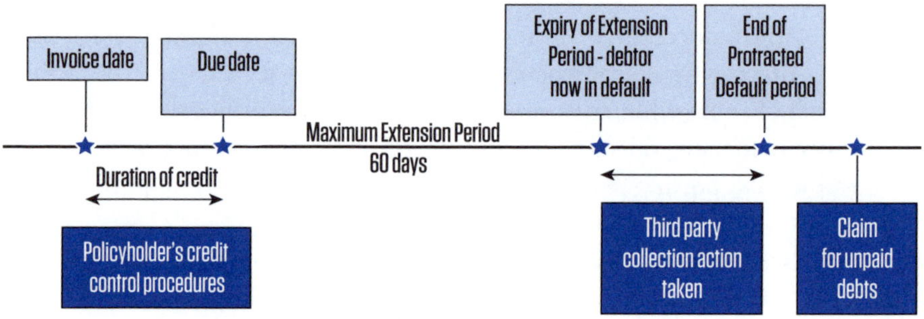

to 60 days when an in-house collections company is being used), and could increase till up to 360 days for high risk countries. In Europe, depending on the country, the protracted default period is in principle no longer than 6 months. We already mentioned that just after the MEP (and thus within the protracted default period) there is the 14 day grace period during which the policyholder has to report an overdue.

The end of the protracted default period (from 60 days up to 360 days depending on the country) is the date of loss, at which date the claim is payable. If insolvency occurs however before the end of the protracted default, the date of insolvency becomes the date of loss.

From this date of loss (thus from the end of the protracted default period or date of insolvency), the policyholder has again another 6 months to submit a claim, but he can do it earlier during this protracted default period which is in fact the collection period. However, the policyholder can prefer to wait to submit this claim within the protracted default context to avoid impacting his loss ratio, and thus try to collect in the meanwhile as much as possible. After the claim submission, the claims assessment period of 30 days starts, at the end of which the compensation is paid (cf. fig. 4.3).

The maximum possible timeline is thus: 60 days (MEP) + protracted default period (60 days up to 360 days, with the 14 days grace period in it at the beginning) + 180 days (maximum period to submit claim) + 30 days to pay a claim after its assessment (see below).
There is thus a clear distinction in the UK between:

- reporting an overdue after the MEP at the beginning of the protracted default period (in the grace period);

- submitting a claim when collection didn't recover everything at the end of the protracted default period (although it can be done earlier as well).

The Euler Hermes Report Collect Claim form is designed so that the policy-holder can report the account as overdue, pass for collection and submit a claim in one process. In practical terms this speeds up the process for clients and means debts are collected / claims are paid much quicker.

1.4 LOSS COMPENSATION

Notwithstanding his prevention and risk procedures, the credit insurer will obviously be confronted from time to time with claims that lead to the payment of loss compensation, when it proves impossible to recover the full amount owed by the debtor.

→ *Cause of loss*

When invoices remain unpaid and the cause is the financial inability of the debtor to meet his obligations, the insured party will have the right to make a claim for compensation in accordance with the terms of his policy. In this respect, a distinction is made between insolvency and protracted default:

- proven insolvency: administration, CVA, liquidation or other equivalent procedures in the country in question;
- failure to pay within the agreed protracted default period (from 60 to 360 days, depending on the country), where there is an assumption that unless a satisfactory recovery programme can be agreed with the buyer, some form of administration or insolvency will follow. Alternatively, in some cases the anticipated costs for recovering a debt can far outweigh the size of the debt itself, therefore making its collection pointless. Moreover, buyers do sometimes simply cease trading and disappear – this is mainly the case with unlimited companies and partnerships.

→ *Why is there a waiting/protracted default period?*

A waiting period serves a number of purposes:

- it gives the parties the opportunity to arrange payment by mutual agreement;
- the insurer only gets involved in cases of actual and (probable) permanent loss;

- it reduces unnecessary administration; for example, after any compensation settlement has been paid, most policies require the recovered funds to be divided between the insurer and the insured party in the same proportion as the loss borne by the two parties following payment of the claim (in other words, if the credit insurer has paid 90% of the loss, he will be entitled to 90% of any recovery).

→ *Determining the amount of compensation*

The compensation must not amount to more than the covered percentage of the applicable and valid credit limit (the agreed indemnity percentage). By insisting that the insured supplier retains the uninsured percentage at his own risk, the insurer seeks to ensure that the supplier will take the monitoring of his default risks and any necessary recovery action seriously.

ATTENTION!

Unless specifically agreed otherwise, the insurer will not be liable for loss in respect of any deliveries made when the buyer is already in default (i.e. beyond the MEP) in respect of earlier deliveries. This same exclusion also applies to deliveries made after the withdrawal of the credit limit. It is generally considered to be wise commercial practice for suppliers to stop deliveries until all previous amounts owing have been paid. The withholding of new deliveries is an obvious first means by which pressure can be applied on the debtor to settle his outstanding invoices. Any payments received after the expiry of the MEP will be allocated to the oldest debt and treated as salvage. This can have a large impact on liability, when the policyholder has traded over their credit limit, since it means that he can be left with a debt which is uninsured.

As figure 4.2 shows, if the debtor is still in default at the expiry of the Maximum Extension Period (usually 60 days after the original date due), all new deliveries are no longer covered by the terms of the policy.

Eventual loss is calculated on the basis of the unpaid invoices that fall within the previously granted credit limit, with the deduction of any credit notes and any payments actually made. VAT is not normally included in the cover. If the VAT due from the buyer is not reimbursed, the insured seller is normally able to claim a credit for his own liability from the tax and revenue authorities.

FIGURE 4.2 *Schedule for delivery stop and termination of cover (source: Euler Hermes)*

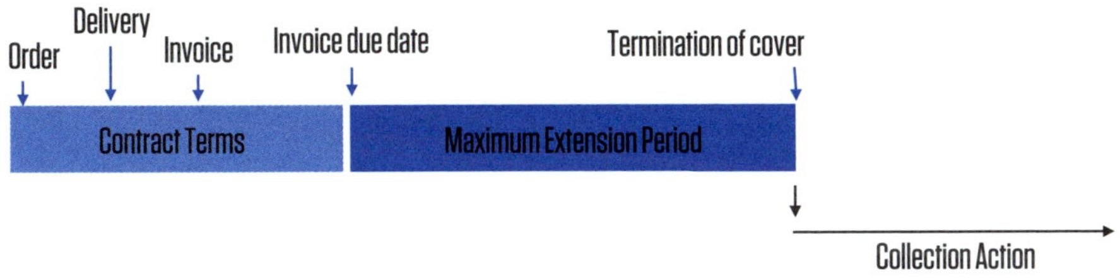

Default interest for late payment and other penalties are not included in the amount paid out for loss compensation. Credit insurers do, however, encourage their policyholders to include these items under their terms and conditions of sale, so that they can be recovered from the debtor by a collection agency. Loss which may occur as a result of fluctuations in rates of exchange is also excluded from the claim. Care should be taken when sales contracts are concluded in a currency other than the currency in which the liability has been expressed under the policy terms. In other words, if a policy is taken out in United Kingdom, where the credit insurer has agreed to accept premiums and pay claims in sterling, sales contracts concluded in any currency other than sterling will face an exchange rate differential in the event of loss. Normally, premiums are paid in sterling at the ruling rate in force at the time of delivery (i.e., when liability under the policy commences), and claims will be met using the same rate of exchange. If the policy provides for pre-delivery cover, then the ruling rate will be the rate in force on the date of the sales contract. Some credit insurers (such as Euler Hermes) use the spot rate of exchange in force in the London foreign exchange market at the close of business on the last working day of the month in which the goods were despatched or services provided.

Another important factor is the allocation of any payments received, including the recoveries (this will be illustrated by an example later in the book):

- most policies foresee that partial payments are first allocated against the principle sum;
- every payment received as an advance against future deliveries is regarded as settlement of the outstanding debt with the oldest expired payment date, unless previously agreed otherwise by the underwriter;
- payments that are received after the expiry of the MEP but prior to the submission of a claim are deducted from the oldest outstanding receivable (salvage). Monies received after the claim submission are divided proportionally between credit insurer and policyholder based on their share in the total loss.

In some cases, third party securities may be involved. These are usually joint surety bonds or retention of title agreements (see below). Before the insurer pays out any compensation, the policy may sometimes stipulate that these securities must first be invoked and that any recoveries made after payment of a claim should be divided proportionally between the parties.

In the event of the claim being contested by the debtor, the supplier (insured party) may attempt:

- to reach a mutual agreement with his customer (debtor);
- if this is not possible, seek to enforce his rights through legal action.

ATTENTION!

If the amount owed by the buyer is contested, the insured party's right to compensation is temporarily suspended. For example, the debtor may argue that the quality of the delivered goods was sub-standard; hence his refusal to pay. In this case, the non-payment is not related to the debtor's ability to pay, so that the intervention of the insurer at this stage is not justified.

If an out-of-court settlement is reached or if a court judgment is given in the seller's favour, there is automatically an agreed debt that was due on the contractual due date. Settlement of a claim becomes payable (in respect of the agreed debt) at the end of the protracted default period set out in the policy document.

The following costs can also be included in the compensation payment:

- costs that form part of the original invoiced amount, (for example, transport and packaging costs);
- costs incurred to pursue or maintain the claim (for example, protest procedures in respect of unpaid bills of exchange);
- collection costs (for example, lawyers' fees, collection agency charges, etc.).

Any costs included in the original invoice are always admissible (provided premium was paid on the total invoice value). The other charges described above will be incurred during the consultation process to determine the appropriate recovery action to be taken and, as such, will require the insurer's prior approval. In general, this is usually given; the insurer simply reserves the right to refuse to sanction costs he considers too high.

Finally, there is the matter of first loss deductibles or excesses. These are the amounts for which the insured party is prepared to carry the risk himself (see below), which normally has the effect of lowering the premium. These exempt amounts are then deducted from any amounts of compensation that need to be paid.

→ *Maximum amount of liability*

In general, the credit insurer will stipulate in the policy a maximum amount of compensation that can be paid in any single insurance year. This amount is usually equivalent to 25 times the minimum premium or the actual premium, if this second amount is higher, but in certain circumstances may be more. This ceiling is applicable to all compensation claims that arise and are payable in respect of the insurance year in question. The ceiling is reset to the maximum level at the beginning of each new insurance year.

→ *Payment*

In principle, the compensation, following calculation in the above manner, is paid 30 days after:

- the recognition of the validity of the claim as a financial liability of the debtor through an official declaration of insolvency; or
- the date of insolvency.

Of course, this presupposes that the loss claim submitted to the insurer by the insured party is fully in order.

FIGURE 4.3 *Schedule for the payment of loss compensation in cases of suspected insolvency (source: Euler Hermes)*

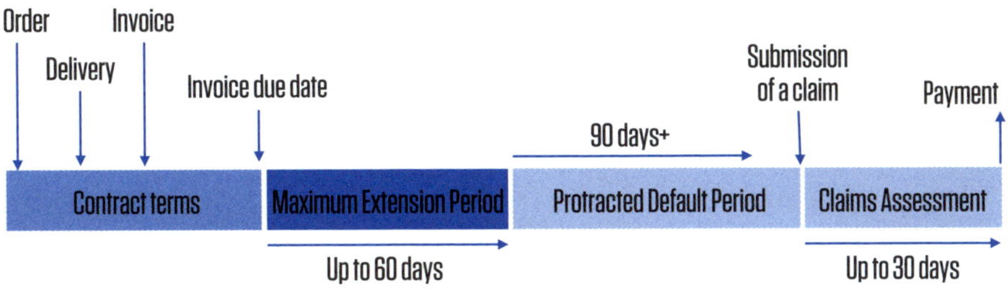

Figure 4.3 shows the order of events for a protracted default claim. It is worth bearing in mind that a claims assessment can be made during the protracted default period so the claim can be paid as soon as possible at the end of the Protracted Default period.

The protracted default period is 90 days (and even 60 days in the UK: see above) for most developed markets but can be up to 360 days for the highest risk markets.

For an insolvency claim, the assessment will be made within 30 days of receipt of the claim form (in either electronic or paper format) and supporting documentation.

→ *Termination of the policy after the payment of compensation*

The credit insurer can, if he so wishes, stipulate in the policy that he has the right to terminate the policy after the payment of a high level of compensation:
- → either after having given 60 days notice to the insured party;
- → or by non-renewal on the annual expiry date.

This option can be viewed in two lights:
- → it can be a signal that there are weaknesses in the internal credit management organisation of the insured supplier;
- → the old policy was unprofitable for the insurer, so that he wishes to use the termination clause as a possible way to renegotiate the policy conditions.

2 Extending the pure commercial risk

In addition to the pure commercial risk, the policy can also be extended to provide the following cover:

2.1 PRE-DELIVERY OR MANUFACTURING RISK

This is cover against the insolvency and protracted default risk involved in the provision of goods and (to a lesser extent) services that are 'made-to-measure'. These are goods that are non-standard and are often to the specific design requirements of the buyer. The value of the goods, in the event of cancellation, would probably be reduced to their scrap value. During the manufacturing process, however, the supplier will already have incurred significant costs relating to these goods. This means that if the customer becomes insolvent before the actual delivery takes place, the supplier can suffer serious financial loss. The non-standard nature of the goods makes it difficult, if not impossible, to recover these costs by sale to a third party.

In such cases, the insured customer can request an additional clause to be included in the policy that covers risks of this kind.

2.2 BINDING CONTRACTS

It can sometimes happen that the credit insurer wishes to reduce or revoke a credit limit, even though the insured customer has no outstanding claims at that particular moment in time. This could put the insured customer in a difficult position, especially if he is unable (either legally or contractually) to withdraw from the delivery commitments he has made, since this would result in him being subject to a damage claim from his buyer/debtor for his failure to meet his agreed obligations. Of course, the supplier would still be at liberty to make the delivery at his own risk (since it would no longer be covered by the insurer).

For this reason, the insured customer obtains that binding contracts will continue to enjoy the previously agreed level of cover, providing the contracts are recent and that the delivery can be completed in a reasonable period of time (usually 3 months after the revised credit decision). This is of particular interest to the construction sector.

There are two further conditions:
- there must be no outstanding arrears beyond the MEP at the moment of reduction/termination;
- there must be a clear legal and/or contractual obligation to make the delivery.

FIGURE 4.4 *Schedule for binding contracts for 3 months (source: Euler Hermes)*
In figure 4.4, orders placed with the insured supplier 3 months before the ter-

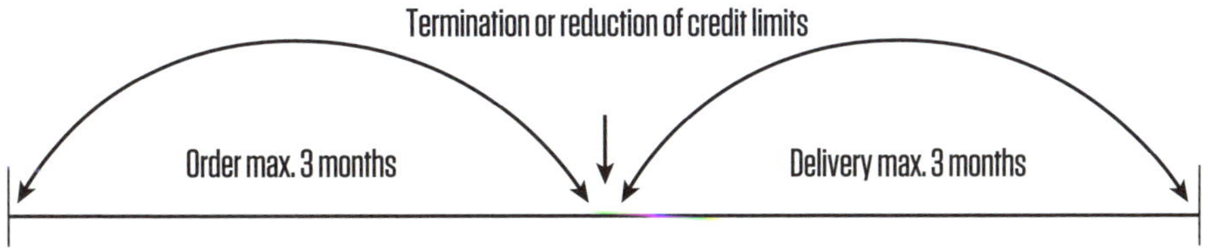

mination or reduction of the credit limit can be completed under continued insurance cover, providing the delivery takes place within 3 months of the date on which the limits were reduced or terminated.

3 Types of credit decision

In terms of credit decisions, it is possible to distinguish four different variants that help to determine the nature and conditions of the credit insurance policy.

3.1 DISCRETIONARY LIMITS

Under the terms and conditions of the policy, a level is agreed within which the insured customer can agree his own credit limits, without reference to the credit insurer. The appropriate level is agreed by underwriters, who have to be satisfied with the company's credit management system (for example, that it automatically takes out credit references from at least one independent source for the amount in question, or monitors how much has previously been outstanding and duly paid by the buyers in question). The agreed level will also reflect the fact that the profile of most companies' buyers will show the largest number of customers falling within the 'smaller' category. If drawn diagrammatically, in the form of a pyramid, the base would be formed of smaller buyers and the peak would represent the largest buyer(s).

Discretionary limits offer two advantages:
- the insured party can save on limit costs, whilst at the same time simplifying his own administration;
- the credit insurer also saves valuable time on what are essentially 'minor' matters.

The use of this system is subject to the following conditions:
- the insured party must not have had past payment difficulties with the customer in question and must not be in possession of negative information about the customer's reputation and/or financial position;
- the policy may stipulate that a previous refusal of a credit limit for the customer in question is equivalent to 'negative information'.

Although a credit insurer's standard indemnity in the UK is 90%, it drops to

70% if a credit reference report or trading experience is used as justification. If the underwriter's own opinions service is used, the indemnity remains at 90%.

ATTENTION!

These discretionary limits within a straightforward whole turnover policy should not be confused with the limits of a different product - the credit management policy (see below) - where the level of discretion is generally much higher and is only agreed after a comprehensive audit of the internal credit management procedures of the insured party has been carried out by the insurers.

3.2 TEMPORARY CREDIT LIMITS

It can sometimes happen that the insurer does not have at his immediate disposal all the information he needs to make his credit decision. Obtaining this information can take time. To show his good faith towards the insured party, the insurer may decide to issue a temporary credit limit, so that covered deliveries can be made without further delay. If the supplementary information requested by the insurer about the customer turns out to be positive, the credit limit can be confirmed as permanent (usually for a higher amount). If the information is negative, the insurer can reduce or even revoke the temporary limit.

3.3 LIMITS OF RESTRICTED DURATION: TEMPORARY INCREASES

GOOD TO KNOW

Sometimes the limit granted for a particular debtor will only be valid for a restricted period. This is an exception to the more typical 'revolving' nature of credit insurance. The temporary increase is a good example of this phenomenon.

Many (if not most) companies are subject to seasonal fluctuations. This means that turnover is not equally distributed over the 12 months of a year. There will be some months when the turnover is considerably higher. This means that the credit limits for some customers may not be sufficient during these months of peak activity.

The credit insurer may decide that the granting of a permanent limit to reflect these seasonal peaks may not be appropriate. (This happens most frequently when the underwriter is faced with tight capacity on a limit, and it allows him to keep within actual usage, rather than leaving spare unused 'fat' in the system.) However, to show his understanding for the insured party's situation, he may opt to temporarily increase the existing limits for a restricted period. This period will coincide with the insured party's 'busy' season. The temporary limits expire at the end of that season and must be requested anew for the following year.

4 Excesses or franchises

'Franchise' is a technical word used by some credit insurance companies to mean that they are 'franchising out' the responsibility for taking losses up to a given point. Other credit insurance companies use the more common insurance term known as 'excess'. There are four types of excess.

4.1 GENERAL EXCESS PER INSURANCE YEAR (AFL=AGGREGATE FIRST LOSS; AA=ANNUAL AGGREGATE)

This excess is applicable to all loss claims in an insurance year.

EXAMPLE

If the excess amounts to 15,000 euros and if the total amount of loss compensation due during that insurance year amounts to 20,000 euros, the credit insurer will only pay out the insured percentage of 5,000 euros to the insured party, this being the amount over the 15,000 euros of aggregate first loss.

4.2 THRESHOLD EXCESS (IFL=INTEGRAL FIRST LOSS; THRESHOLD)

This type of excess implies that loss compensation/claims will only be paid when the amount of the claim exceeds an agreed minimum amount (or threshold).

EXAMPLE
Imagine that the threshold is £500. If the insured party submits a loss claim for £400, the insurer pays nothing. If the insured party submits a loss claim for £600, the insurer pays out the insured percentage of the £600 in compensation.

4.3 EXCESS PER CLAIM (EEFL=EACH AND EVERY FIRST LOSS)

This type of excess requires the insured party to bear the agreed amount of the excess for each instance of loss.

EXAMPLE
If the amount of the excess is 500 euros and the amount of the loss claim is 2,000 euros, the insurer will only pay out the insured percentage on 1,500 euros as compensation to the insured party. For a following claim of 3,000 euros, he would pay out the insured percentage on 2,500 euros in compensation, etc.

4.4 MINIMUM RETENTION

This type of excess deducts either the excess level or the uninsured percentage, whichever is the greater.

EXAMPLE
If the excess level is £500, with 90% insured level, for a claim of £4,000, the claim value will be £3,500 (the £500 excess is removed). If the claim is for £6,000, the claim value will be £5,400 (the 10% uninsured percentage is removed).

5 Costs for the insured party

The insured party incurs three different kinds of costs in respect of his credit insurance policy.

5.1 THE PREMIUM

The premium can be paid annually, quarterly or monthly in advance, depending on the conditions specified in the policy. It is calculated by applying a premium rate to the turnover figures supplied by the insured party. The minimum premium is retained in all circumstances, but other premium refunds can be given where turnover fails to reach the estimated levels.

→ ***Premium rate***

GOOD TO KNOW

In contrast to most general insurance products, the premium is designed to cover what is essentially a variable risk: this year's good debtor may (for various reasons) turn out to be next year's bad risk. In European legislation, credit insurance risks are classified as being 'high risk'. As a result, they are subject to the setting aside of a greater number of technical provisions within insurance company accounts. The amounts of these provisions (for example, the equalisation provision) are usually set on the basis of statistical and actuarial calculations, with the aim of ensuring that sufficient financial reserves are available to pay out potential loss claims. These provisions are shown on the liabilities side of the annual account and contribute towards the continuing solvency of the insurer, to the benefit of his insured parties.

The premium is expressed as a percentage of the insured turnover. Most premiums vary between fractions of 0.1% and as much as 1%.

The precise level of premium is subject to a number of different factors:
- the scope of the insurance: for example, does it cover just official insolvency, or also protracted default (suspected insolvency), political risks, etc.?
- the risk period: for example, does it cover pre-delivery (manufacturing) risks, as well as delivery risks?
- the nature of the risks: for example, do they include binding contracts cover?
- the trade sector in which the risks are being run;
- the average payment period;
- the risk spread within the customer's portfolio;
- the loss statistics for the previous year: when the policy is a new one, the supplier is required to draw up a summary of all the losses, caused by the default of his customers on accounts receivable, which he has incurred during the past three years; the insurer can then form an opinion about the prospective

customer's credit control procedures and also decide whether his own preventative procedures might have been able to avoid or reduce these losses.

The prospective customer (the future insured party) is obliged to provide all this information. The details are usually given on a standard proposal form (see appendix 2). Where they are monitored in automatic systems, the ratings given to the debtors within the prospective customer's buyer portfolio are often the key element in the premium calculation. In this way, the insurer is provided with an accurate picture of the risk profile. And the greater the risk, the higher the premium.

The premium is calculated on the basis of the insurable turnover under the terms and conditions of the policy. To make this possible, the insured party must submit regular updates of his turnover figures.

The premium rate is also influenced by the other factors mentioned earlier: bonus-malus (no claims bonus), percentage of cover, type and level of excess (franchise), etc.

In addition, a fixed-rate premium can be calculated for certain types of policy. These are sometimes policies for very small companies, but are more commonly credit management policies for larger clients.

→ *Notification of turnover*

The insured party must notify the total of his insurable turnover under the terms and conditions of the policy (turnover policy), and this per country and per currency, with full details of the length of the credit period.

Risks that have been excluded from the policy do not need to be declared. These exclusions, to which we referred earlier, include:

- → any invoiced amounts of VAT (usually excluded);
- → invoices for government bodies in OECD countries;
- → confirmed irrevocable letters of credit;
- → cash payments;
- → the turnover of companies over which the insured party exercises effective control (e.g., shareholder, membership in board of directors, etc.);
- → private individuals who do not have the status of a 'trader';
- → invoices for debtors who have been rejected by the credit insurer on the basis of refused credit limits.

This process (whereby the insured customer is required to submit actual turnover figures to the credit insurer, including details of the amounts for each debtor) has been revised or simplified by some credit insurers. It is now possible in many cases for a turnover prognosis to be made when the policy is first taken out. This forms the basis for the calculation of the premium, as shown in figure 4.5. At the end of each policy year the insured party provides an annual declaration, which summarises his actual turnover figures for the previous 12 months. This is then used to calculate a final premium for the completed policy year.

It is self-evident that this declaration is a crucial element for the effective working of the policy. The credit insurer has the right to check the figures, if he has reason to doubt their accuracy. The late or incorrect notification of the figures may impact the cover granted under the policy.

Declarations are due within 60 days of the agreed declaration period. If they have not been received by then, the credit insurer is entitled to withhold claim payments. If subsequent attempts (letters of reminder, etc.) fail to obtain the required declarations, the insurer may decide to terminate the policy.

FIGURE 4.5 *Schedule for the notification of turnover figures (source: Euler Hermes)*

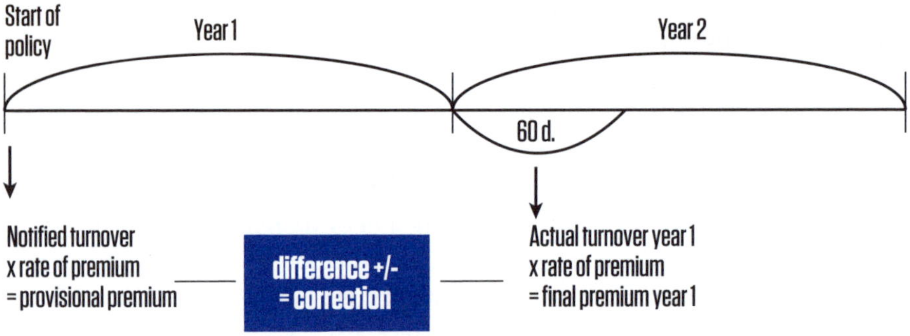

FIGURE 4.6 *Schedule for the non-notification of turnover figures (source: Euler Hermes)*

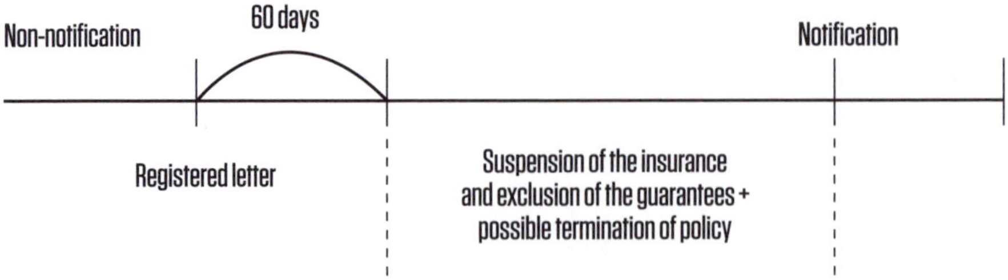

→ *Negotiating the rate of premium*

If a potential customer regards the rate of premium as being too high, he can seek alternative quotations, which might reduce the rate by applying one of the following measures, all of which increase the customer's retention of risk:

- → lowering the percentage of cover;
- → accepting higher excesses of loss (franchises – see above);
- → the limiting of the risk period (for example, by taking out policies for specific eventualities: pre-delivery risks, binding contracts cover, etc.).

It may be possible for long-term policyholders to agree a bonus-malus clause, which means that the insured party shares in the good or bad performance of the policy. This often allows a lower rate of premium to be granted, but one which will be automatically increased if the level of loss becomes too high in relation to the premium. This latter calculation is made as follows:

- → the insurer books (as a credit) the premiums paid by the insured party over a particular period;
- → the insurer books (as a debit) both his general costs (usually estimated at about 30% of the premium) and the net payments of loss compensation (after deduction of recoveries) in respect of claims made during the same period;
- → the balance of these two transactions is the technical result of the policy and determines the level of bonus-malus.

The same method of calculating the technical result of the policy is used to determine the insured party's participation in any profit accruing from the policy or for the award of a premium rebate of between 20 and 30% to the insured party, when the technical result is positive. The specific details of the calculation method will generally be included in the policy.

GOOD TO KNOW

The technical result of an insurance company for its core insurance activity is (roughly) the same as the operating result (earnings before interest and tax) of a commercial company. The best gauge of technical profitability is the so-called combined ratio. This expresses compensations and operating costs as a percentage of the premium income. As long as the combined ratio remains under 100%, it is possible to speak of technical profit.

→ *Annual minimum premium*

This is the lowest amount that the insured party must pay each year, irrespective of other factors; even, for example, if the estimated insurable turnover is not realised. In general, this minimum premium is usually 90% of the estimated annual premium.

The reasons for setting a minimum level of premium are:
- → a lower level of income from the policy would mean that the insurer is not being sufficiently compensated for the risks he is required to take; after all, it is possible that he may incur loss from the very first day of the policy;
- → the insurer also has fixed costs that he needs to cover;
- → the insurer can still demand payment of this premium in the year that the policy is terminated by the insured party;
- → the insurer hopes to discourage the attempts of insured parties to secure a lower rate of premium by notifying exaggerated turnover predictions.

During the financial and economic crisis of 2008-2009 there was some criticism of this practice. The turnover of some insured companies fell dramatically because of the reduced level of economic activity, the cutting down of stocks (to create greater liquidity) and the dramatic fall in the price of raw materials. As a result, the insured turnover of some companies fell below the level of the minimum premium, which they were still required to pay, notwithstanding the difficult economic circumstances.

→ *Sanctions for the non-payment of the premium*

The credit insurer can refuse to grant further permanent cover if the insured party fails to pay his premium. In these circumstances, credit insurers first withhold claim payments, whilst simultaneously chasing up the premium. Termination of the policy is a last resort.

GOOD TO KNOW

This procedure is justified by the fact that in credit insurance it is often possible for an insured party to take account of a loss he suspects is likely to happen in the near future. The insurer wants to prevent the insured party from waiting for this loss to occur, so that he can offset payment of the premium against it and thereby re-activate the policy.

FIGURE 4.7 *Schedule for the non-payment of premium (source: Euler Hermes)*

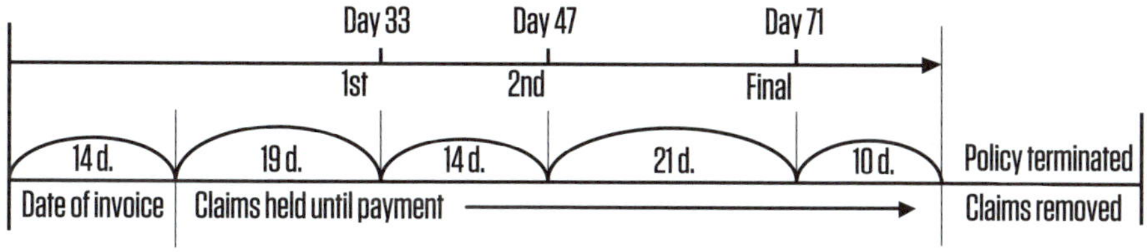

If the premium is not received within 14 days from the date of the invoice, claim payments are withheld. On day 33 the insurer will send a chaser letter for the outstanding amount, with a further chaser on day 47. A final demand letter is issued on day 71, which advises the insured party to pay the outstanding amount within 10 days; otherwise the policy will be terminated without liability for any claims (figure 4.7).

5.2 LIMIT COSTS

These costs are sometimes also referred to as study costs. They are the second of the three costs of the policy (premium and collection costs being the others). They are recompense for the costs incurred by the insurer for the collection (and purchase) of the information necessary to analyse the credit application submitted by the insured party and to carry out risk monitoring of the existing limits. VAT is charged on limit fees, which is more advantageous for clients than insurance premium tax.

There are two types of limit costs:

1. Costs for limit applications: each application is invoiced separately; the costs are not usually applied to applications for the increase of existing limits, since the insurer is already familiar with the case and the insured party is already paying a fee in respect of this debtor in the form of monitoring costs.
2. Costs for monitoring: invoices are drawn up for each debtor, as long as the insured party holds a credit limit on that particular debtor.

Limit application costs are invoiced at the end of the month in which the application for credit on a debtor was made to the insurer. The monitoring costs in respect of this debtor are paid monthly in arrears.

When a limit is revoked by the insurer or a limit is cancelled by the insured party, the monitoring costs will cease with effect from the start of the following month.

The level of the costs varies, dependent on the country in which the debtor is located and on whether the costs relate to an application or to monitoring. Special policies (such as those from SMEs) often include a fixed-rate annual fee based on a specific number of limits that is set when the policy is first drawn up.

The tasks carried out for the insured party are a service and are therefore subject to the payment of VAT. However, the insured party can show this VAT as a deduction in his normal company return.

Because of this 'service' aspect, the invoices for limit costs are usually invoiced by a separate service company, set up by the credit insurer specifically for this purpose. This company manages the risk database and is responsible for gathering and analysing the information about the debtors covered by insurer.

BE SMART

In order to reduce his limit fee costs, an insured party can:

- → cancel the limits he no longer needs;
- → make his own 'monitoring' assessments within the framework of the discretionary limits procedure.

5.3 COLLECTION COSTS

In section 1.4 of this chapter (the section on loss compensation) we have already seen that collection costs – the expenses incurred by the insurer or the insured party to recoup unpaid debts covered by the policy – can also be included in the policy cover. However, the insurer must approve these expenses before payment (to guard against waste and/or exaggeration). Only a percentage of the costs are covered, so that some portion always remains the responsibility of the insured party.

If the credit insurer accepts responsibility for the collection costs but no result is realised, this will lead to a significant reduction in the commission fee. If there is no specific mention of cover in the policy, the collection costs are a charge against the insured party.

Debt collection is a service and therefore subject to the payment of VAT.

5.4 FISCAL PROCEDURES RELATING TO INSURANCE PREMIUMS, OTHER COSTS AND LOSS COMPENSATION

It is generally accepted that the premium is tax deductible in full. This is not the case for a bad-debt provision. These provisions are therefore financial reserves to protect the company from unforeseen losses caused by the non-payment of its invoices.

→ ***Insurance premiums and other costs (collection and study costs)***

The (credit) insurance premiums (as well as collection costs, limit costs and monitoring costs) all comply with the definition of professional expenses, in the sense that the expenses are incurred with the intention of acquiring or protecting the income of that profession or undertaking.

For companies, however, it is important that the so-called 'one year accruals' principle is respected. This means that companies, which pay charges in a certain financial year, must sometimes book these charges as costs (either in part or in full) via their accruals to the following financial year. If, for example, the annual credit insurance premium is paid in advance on 1 July 2012, providing cover for the turnover of the insured party from 1 July 2012 to 30 June 2013, half the premium must be booked as a cost against the 2013 financial year via the accruals account.

→ ***Loss compensation***

Where deduction of the credit insurance premium is allowable against tax, any loss compensation received by the insured party from an insurer will, in general, be regarded as taxable professional income.

It is also important to remember that any residual loss relating to trade receivables over and above any loss compensation will normally be allowed as a tax deductible professional expense. However, the loss first has to be certain and fixed. It must also be booked in the annual accounts, even if it is not actually realised.

6 Use factor

6.1 WHAT IS THE USE FACTOR?

For reasons of efficiency, the insured customer does not need to submit a detailed schedule of covered turnover per debtor. This means, however, that the credit insurer cannot know with any precision to what extent the nominal credit limits are actually being used.

Over time, the credit limits that have been agreed by the credit insurer can fall into partial or even full disuse (e.g. when a debtor ceases to buy from an insured supplier). Consequently, the risk of non-payment no longer exists and the insured customer no longer requires the credit limit granted by the insurer. Nevertheless, if the insured party fails to notify this to the insurer, the limit will remain open.

It is generally accepted that only about 30% of a credit insurer's agreed credit limits are actually in use at any one time. This is known as the use factor.

6.2 THE IMPORTANCE OF THE USE FACTOR

For a credit insurer, ascertaining the actual use factor can be important in the following instances:

- → for assessing the efficiency of the operational use of the nominal credit limits;
- → for negotiating with reinsurers;
- → for the obligatory calculation of the insurer's own capital needs, on the basis of the actual outstanding risk portfolio (also known as the risk allocated capital or RAC);
- → for the calculation of the theoretical premium for the policyholder, by using a pricing model based on the actual risks being covered (i.e. limits which are actually being used); this is much better than a calculation based on nominal risks, since this might include a number of limits no longer being used, which could skew the pricing one way or the other.

Summary of the respective obligations of the insured party and the credit insurer

In contrast to a general insurance policy, a credit insurance policy requires a dynamic approach from both parties.

OBLIGATIONS OF THE INSURED CUSTOMER

The insured customer is responsible for the following matters:
- ensuring the correct procedures (e.g. obtaining credit reports) are in place, in order to justify amounts that will be outstanding from buyers under the agreed level of discretion;
- applying for credit limits for his buyers, above the discretionary limit level;
- the periodic notification of his insurable turnover figures;
- the payment of the premium and associated fees;
- the notification to the insurer of any adverse information about his covered debtors, as soon as he becomes aware of it;
- linked to this last point, the periodic notification of past due accounts receivable; this must take place within a pre-determined period of time;
- the prompt transfer of any recoveries in respect of these outstanding accounts receivable.

OBLIGATIONS OF THE INSURER

As with any company, there are two different types of task: sensu stricto and sensu lato:

→ *Sensu stricto (in the strict sense)*

On the basis of the agreed policy, the insurer is responsible for the following tasks:
- granting credit limits, once he has completed a creditworthiness analysis;
- justifying the rejection or partial granting of applications for credit limits; this applies equally if credit limits are later revoked or reduced;
- the payment of loss compensation in respect of claims made by the insured party on the basis of the cover percentage specified in the policy.

→ ***Sensu lato*** ***(in the broad sense)***

It is important for the credit insurer to provide high levels of service to the insured customer. In particular, the insurance policy is obliged to support the insured customer's own credit management activities. In order to test his performance levels, the insurer uses a series of key indicators, which are monitored and reported on a regular basis. For example:

- answer-times for credit applications: the insured customer needs a quick response to his request, so that he can complete his commercial negotiations with his buyer (the debtor);
- the acceptance rate for credit limit applications: the insured customer wants the maximum number of his applications to be dealt with positively, so that he can be fully covered in his business dealings with his buyers (debtors);
- speed of payment for loss compensation: this is vital to allow the insured customer to maintain his liquidity position.

Practical example for the settlement of a loss claim

In this paragraph, we will look at an example where an insured party has submitted a claim for loss compensation to his insurer in respect of the insolvency of a buyer for whom he had been granted a credit limit. This example is used to illustrate the various issues described above. It would be very unusual for all of the issues raised in the example to occur within a single claim, but they are used here for illustrative purposes only. It must, of course, be remembered that there will always be differences between the policies of different insurance companies. Consequently, it is always important to examine the details of each individual policy carefully.

A) PRINCIPLES

The following are the most important principles when dealing with a contested claim.

→ *Principles relating to loss compensation*

1 The loss compensation paid to the insured customer can never exceed the cover percentage of the agreed credit limit, reduced with any other relevant deductions (such as excesses, etc.). No account is taken of VAT, since VAT is not (generally) a covered risk (because VAT can be recovered by the insured party from the VAT administration).
2 Deliveries made after the known likelihood of an impending loss or after the withdrawal of a credit limit are not eligible for compensation.
3 Compensation for collection costs will be paid if the principle sum is covered.
4 A dispute (most frequently in respect of the quality of the delivery) will result in a suspension of the right to compensation until the dispute has been resolved.

→ *Recovery*

The method of working is dependent on the manner in which the claim is submitted. If the recovery takes place before the submission of the compensation claim, the invoice with the oldest date of due payment will be the first to be cleared or paid. This means that if the insured party recovers partial payment from the debtor before he submits a claim (which applies generally in relation to the expiring of the protracted default period), this will simply reduce the overall amount of the outstanding debt – and therefore the claim.

If recovery is made after the claim has been submitted and paid, the amounts in question are divided proportionally between the insured party and the insurer in relation to their individual share in the loss.

→ ***Policy conditions***

If the policy conditions have not been complied with fully, the right to compensation may be lost, either in part or in whole.

B) CASE STUDY: DESCRIPTION AND DEFINITION OF THE PROBLEM

→ ***The following elements are relevant to this case:***

- → The insured party has a global policy and is therefore covered against both official insolvency and protracted default (suspected insolvency).
- → The cover percentage is 90%.
- → The invoice payment conditions are 30 days after the invoice date.
- → The credit limit granted by the credit insurer amounts to 50,000 euros.
- → The claim of the supplier (insured customer) against his buyer (debtor) relates to three invoices:
  - an invoice of 10 March for an amount of 25,000 euros;
  - an invoice of 15 April for an amount of 30,000 euros;
  - an invoice of 15 June for an amount of 25,000 euros.
- → The debtor pays the sum of 2,500 euros on 15 June.
- → The insured customer submits his compensation claim to the insurer on 20 June.
- → The debtor is officially declared insolvent by the commercial court on 19 August.
- → The insurer pays out compensation to the insured customer on 18 September. The rule is that under protracted default a claim would in general be payable on 9 September, i.e. 90 days from the end of MEP (8 June). (Protracted default periods vary from 60 days in the UK to 90 or 180 days for other countries, but 270 and 360 days are also possible in the event that commercial cover has been given in high risk markets). As insolvency occured on 19 August a claim would be payable from this 9 September.
- → Through the application of the retention of title principle, a further 10,000 euros is recovered on 10 October.
- → In this case, no account is taken of recovery costs.

→ *Definition of the problem*

We will focus on two specific aspects:

- → What is the final amount of loss compensation paid out by the insurer?
- → What is the real loss for the insured party, following deduction of the recoveries?

c) CASE STUDY: SOLUTION

→ *Calculation/payment of loss compensation*

Total amount outstanding: - invoice 10 March: 25,000 - invoice 15 April: 30,000 - invoice 15 June: 25,000	+ 80,000
Received payment on 15 June: This payment was received before the submission of the loss claim and is therefore deducted integrally from the principle sum (no *pro rata* sharing)	- 2,500
	+ 77,500
Non-covered deliveries, made after debtor's first default: The invoice of 15 June is not eligible for cover, since the first invoice of 10 March remained unpaid after 90 days (i.e., 8 June). This 90 day period reflects a normal payment period of 30 days for the invoice, plus a further average period of 60 days delay, during which the insured party remains responsible for chasing up the debtor (MEP). The delivery on 15 June therefore took place after a threat of loss (or state of default) was evident, which leads to a delivery or coverage stop. The preparation/submission of a loss claim took place on 20 June, within the 14 days grace term that started on 8 June and which came to an end on 22 June (an overdue has to be reported).	- 25,000
	+52,500
Exceeding credit limit: The insured party only had a credit limit of 50,000 euros for this debtor.	- 2,500
	+ 50,000
The loss compensation was paid on 18 September, in accordance with the cover percentage of 90%.	**+ 45,000**

→ *Calculation of the insured party's real loss (after proportional sharing of the recoveries)*

1 The proportional share in the loss for both the insurer and the insured party are calculated on the basis of the situation at the moment when the loss compensation was paid:

Share	**Amount**
Credit insurer: amount of loss compensation paid	45,000
Insured party: total loss at the moment when loss compensation was paid: 80,000 – 2,500. The amount that was paid by the debtor/buyer on 15 June (before submission of the loss claim) is deducted from the total outstanding amount.	77,500
The share of the insured party is therefore the difference between: - the credit insurer's share; - the total loss at the moment when loss compensation was paid.	32,500
Credit insurer's share: 45,000/77,500	58.06%
Insured party's share: 32,500/77,500	41.94%

2 Recovery via ownership retention of returned goods (10,000 euros), 41.94% of which is refundable to the insured customer.

Insured party's share of the recoveries: 41.94 % of 10,000.	4,194
Insured party's real loss: The amount still outstanding after payment of loss compensation (32,500) less any share in the recoveries (4,194)	**28,306**

CHAPTER 5
INFORMATION AS THE BASIS FOR GOOD CREDIT DECISIONS

In order to make informed credit decisions, a credit insurer needs reliable information. The database where this information is stored is the power-house behind the entire credit insurance operation. The information is obtained from both published and unpublished sources, and contains country, trade sector and company details.

HOW YOU CAN AVOID PROBLEMS

No company can take good decisions without the correct information. Similarly, no credit insurer can agree credit limits or set accurate ratings without the right data. Most of the time company financial information will be obtained from published sources or from information agencies. However, there can be circumstances where this is insufficient, so that more detailed, confidential information is required. Invariably, this can only be obtained directly from the company (debtor) concerned. It can only be to that company's advantage to co-operate with the credit insurer. After all, the information is being sought because the credit insurer *wants* to agree requested credit limits.

In this chapter we will look at some of the methods the credit insurer uses to make a credit analysis of a company. The focus will be placed on commercial risk; political risks will only be described in general terms.

1 Why should a company give information to a credit insurer?

Information that is obtained directly from a company (as a debtor) is vitally important. This is regarded as proprietary information by the credit insurer.

1.1 DEBTOR RELUCTANCE TO DIVULGE INFORMATION

Debtor companies are sometimes initially reluctant to give information to a credit insurer, because no commercial relationship exists between them. Perhaps they also do not understand why co-operation can only improve their position. Particularly in cases where the credit insurer is faced with adverse information (whether in the public domain or not), it may be helpful for the company to demonstrate directly to the credit insurer that it is aware of the problem and has a plan of action to combat its effect. The credit insurer might decide that this plan is worth supporting and therefore be prepared to continue providing cover. This might be the case, for example, when regular reviews are in place to ensure that bank lending covenants are not in danger of being breached. If the buyer is an off-shore company registered in a tax-efficient country, the only way the credit insurer can obtain information is from the company itself.

HOW IT WORKS

It is possible that debtor companies may only come into contact with a credit insurer as a result of a negative decision (refusal, reduction or withdrawal of a credit limit). In these instances, discretion and diplomacy on the part of credit insured customers and their credit insurer are key to the limiting of any potential damage to business relationships. It is also the best way to obtain additional information that will continue to support the ongoing relationships. Public companies as debtors quoted on stock exchanges are not allowed to provide market-sensitive information selectively. Credit insurers fully understand this and can overcome the problem by signing confidentiality agreements, or by concentrating on issues that are not stock-price sensitive.

European law states that incorporated companies are legally obliged to file their annual accounts with the registrars in the country in which they are registered. These accounts must be made available to the public domain. Penalties may be enforced for late filings.

In 2009 and 2010, the European arm of Euler Hermes wrote to a number of companies in Belgium, asking them to provide information about their figures for the 2008 and 2009 financial years, and also to give some indication about how they were coping with the effect of the financial crisis. Normally, the annual accounts in Belgium are only finalised and submitted in the late summer of the following year (in the UK this is 9 months from the end of the company's financial year-end), but the severity of the 2008-2009 financial and economic crisis meant that the credit insurance sector needed to receive this information as soon as possible (see section 1.3 below).

Letters were sent to the insurer's biggest risks – some 11,000 companies in all. The response rate was just 12%. And the information received was almost entirely from companies that were riding the storm successfully. It seemed that there were no poor results in Belgium that year! It was a different story, however, when the accounts were formally filed with the authorities some months later. This unwillingness to cooperate was a pity, since it meant that credit insurers were probably forced at that time into a harder position than they would otherwise have chosen, because of the widespread failure of companies to provide relevant information.

GOOD SENSE

Credit insurers must always be able to justify any negative decisions they take. If they fail to do this, it can only lead to frustration and a breakdown of respect between the various parties. This justification must be communicated clearly and efficiently.

1.2 THE IMPORTANCE OF PROVIDING INFORMATION

This is to the advantage of the debtor.

GOOD TO KNOW

The buyer can always get more supplier credit if the credit insurer is willing to support him. In particular, companies in difficulties should be aware of the importance of the continued backing of a credit insurer. If this backing is withdrawn, the need for working capital increases, since the level of supplier credit has been reduced. This forces companies to turn to short-term external credit options, which are often very expensive (see below: part IV: return and importance). It is sad to note that some companies are only willing to communicate better with the insurers when they find themselves in serious need. It would be better for mutual trust if all companies were prepared to regard the credit insurers as worthy professional partners.

But it works to the advantage of the credit insurer as well, because it allows him to accept more risks on a reliable and well-founded basis, whilst at the same time supporting the business development of his customer (the insured supplier).

1.3 WHAT INFORMATION DOES THE DEBTOR NEED TO PROVIDE?

USEFUL TIPS

The more information he has, the better the credit insurer is able to make an accurate assessment of the risks. The information he needs will depend (amongst other things) on the creditworthiness of the debtor and the context. Always try to answer the credit insurer's request for information. If in difficulty, request a meeting.

Self-evidently, the risks posed by weak debtors are monitored more closely and the credit insurer needs to receive up-to-date information on these debtors promptly and regularly. This usually means the quarterly figures of the management accounts.

It could be said that the crisis of 2008-2009 was caused by the financial difficulties of the banks: there was a lack of clear understanding about the levels of indebtedness and/or the true asset valuations of the derivative markets, which led to the banks' capital reserves being questioned – which in turn led to major withdrawals of liquidity in normal commercial lending. This inevitably had a negative knock-on effect on the funding and liquidity position of the commercial sector. Business confidence drained away, as did sales turnover. The result of lower sales and restricted bank lending was a serious cash drain. In these circumstances, it was not unreasonable for credit insurers to ask for information about:

- the structure of the companies' bank credits; in particular, the long-term expiry dates;
- the companies' commitments for short-term credits, for which a commitment fee had been paid to the bank; this meant that in the event of liquidity problems, the companies could be sure that the banks would be able to make the necessary credit available to them;
- covenants and conditions that were attached to these credit lines; this was important, since the credit could in theory be legally withdrawn if the covenant is broken; an example of a simple covenant is that a solvency level of 25% (equity capital as a proportion of the total balance) must be maintained; many covenants of this kind were broken during the crisis, but this did not necessarily mean that the banks withdrew the credit facilities; instead, they opted to increase their credit margins by a significant amount.

In addition, credit insurers also ask fundamental questions about developments in the sector, market conditions, budget prospects, etc. In this respect, credit insurers do not differ so much from banks.

1.4 CONFIDENTIALITY

All information received that is not already in the public domain is treated as confidential. When circumstances warrant the need for further detailed information, credit insurers can offer non-disclosure agreements.

2 Database

Underwriting commercial risk is a highly skilled function. An understanding of corporate finance, balance sheets and trading accounts must be allied to considerable experience in judging the quality of corporate management and sound business strategies. However, the growing size and scale of a credit insurer's operations, combined with the need to respond to customer requirements swiftly and efficiently, has made it essential for sophisticated computer systems to be designed and built. These systems meet most day-to-day challenges and otherwise assist in the continuing manual input of underwriting skills. Having said this, while most of the credit insurer's systems are increasingly automated, their actual risk assessment process is still largely carried out manually in their risk underwriting departments. This process is enhanced by risk office information gathering.

Essentially, a credit insurer's IT system consists of a centrally-held database of information and an underwriting system that allows its underwriters around the world not only to access and update the system, but also to record all decisions and calculations made.

2.1 HIGH INVESTMENT COSTS

As already mentioned, the database is the driving force of a credit insurer's business, and is probably the most important item amongst his non-tangible assets. The collection of reliable information is essential:

- to make an accurate assessment of the default risk and to limit potential loss in instances where the information is negative;

GOOD TO KNOW

A database of this kind requires a considerable investment, but remains a key element in the insurer's preventative role. The process of consolidation in the credit insurance sector has led to a number of mergers and acquisitions. This has made possible the creation of large, unified databases for these new credit insurance groups. Cost-efficient synergies have resulted from this larger scale of operations.

- to allow the insurer to take more 'realistic' risks and so increase the level of acceptance for credit applications, which means a better service for the insured parties;
- to give confidence to the credit insurer's own bankers and reinsurers with regard to the insurer's own liabilities and risk capital ratios, etc.

2.2 STRUCTURED AND UNSTRUCTURED DATA

Two types of information are collected and stored in the database.

- Unstructured data: for example, reports of company visits to debtors, reports of telephone enquiries with various stakeholders, other 'loose' information obtained from third parties (press, professional associations, etc.); by using a system of codification, relevant sections of this information are converted into a structured form.
- Structured data: these details are entered into the database via bulk loading or web-services in a ready-structured form.

Structured data is of vital importance, since it is immediately available and suitable for processing (for example, for the development of a scoring model). Moreover, this processing is automated and therefore highly efficient.

2.3 PROPRIETARY AND PROCURED INFORMATION

The information stored in the database is usually obtained in one of two ways: it is either the result of self-investigation (proprietary information) or it is purchased from the sellers of information (procured information).

→ *Proprietary information: the development of a network*

A credit insurer can obtain information in a variety of different ways, such as company visits to buyers/debtors, contact with other company colleagues in overseas risk offices, etc. This is an important type of information, since it allows the insurer to look behind the cold, bald figures recorded in the annual accounts. What is the quality of the company management? Is the long-term strategy sound? Because the insurer collects this proprietary information himself, it is not available to the general public at the moment of its collection (for example, intermediary results, liquidity planning, budget projections, etc.). In contrast, public information is information that is officially published and therefore available to everyone.

For the collection of proprietary information, it is crucial to develop a wide and effective network of contacts. For example, the 'Big Three' credit insurers have extensive international risk office networks, whose principal task is to monitor relevant buyers in their area.

Accountants, trade sector organisations, local chambers of commerce and insurance brokers are all essential networking informants.

→ ***Procured information (from commercial information agencies)***

There are numerous independent agencies in every country selling commercial information for profit. Internationally, the most well known are e.g. Graydon, Experian and Dun & Bradstreet, but there are many others. One credit insurer, Coface, has attempted vertical integration in the sector, through the acquisition of information agencies in all the countries where it operates. But this strategy has recently come to an end.

3 Creditworthiness analysis

The word 'credit' derives from the Latin word *credere*, meaning 'to believe' or 'to trust'. This last word is important: if we offer companies credit, it means that we trust them and their management. However, this trust is based on a series of analytical techniques.

3.1 POLITICAL RISKS

In chapter 1 we gave a broad definition of political risks (risks related to a specific country; please also see chapter 6, section 4.3). In principle, the creditworthiness of a company can never be better than the creditworthiness of its country. This is referred to as the 'sovereign ceiling'.

Generally, country or political risks are assessed in such a way as to produce a country rating. We will be looking at this again in section 4 of chapter 6.

3.2 COMMERCIAL RISKS: THE ANALYTICAL PRINCIPLES

When assessing the creditworthiness of debtors, credit insurers apply straightforward principles of financial analysis, based on the annual trading accounts of the company in question.

We will not be investigating the process of financial analysis in full: there are plenty of other textbooks that cover these matters in more detail. Instead, we will briefly examine some of the key elements from the perspective of credit insurance.

The analysis makes use of both quantitative and qualitative details. For smaller companies there is usually less quantitative information available (for example, published annual accounts), so that the qualitative information becomes correspondingly more important. The weight that is attached to this qualitative information can be varied according to the size of the company, (ranging, for example, from 80% for small companies to 20% for medium-sized companies and 10% for large companies).

The following criteria are the most important for the monitoring of existing credit limits.

→ *Consistency*

The credit insurer applies consistency rules in relation to previous credit decisions. He cannot be seen to favour one insured company over another. This means that if the insurer has granted a limit in respect of a particular buyer to an insured customer in the past, there is a presumption that he will grant the same request in the same circumstances for any other insured customer. Obviously, however, any new information will need to be taken into account.

If, for example, the underwriter is faced with three separate applications for a similar product, an assumption may be made (especially if the product involved is broadly the same) that three competing suppliers are fighting for the same business. In this case, agreement to three separate applications for 500,000 euros would probably involve an actual exposure of no more than 500,000 euros. On the other hand, if the products involved are entirely different, this assumption would change and the real exposure could be as much as 1.5 million euros. Credit insurers generally consider themselves obligated to treat all policyholders fairly, and therefore will usually overcome possible conflicts of interest by issuing temporary limits, until the position becomes clearer.

→ *The general economic climate and the commercial environment*

The general economic climate reflects the current economic cycle. It is logical that in times of economic prosperity there will be relatively fewer insolvencies than during a recession.

As far as the commercial environment is concerned, three factors are relevant:

- the sector: some sectors are more susceptible to insolvency/bankruptcy than others (for example, catering);
- capital requirements: different types of activity require different levels of capital support; for example, a trading company, which is constantly engaged in buying and selling, may experience wide differences in its turnover levels, depending on the success or otherwise of its sales force; in general, this leads to a less robust level of solvency (equity capital as a proportion of the total balance); at the opposite extreme, industry needs a more robust level of solvency, as a cushion against the large investments that need to be made in machines and infrastructure;
- the geographical location: some regions are economically backward, resulting in a greater number of insolvencies.

Annexes of the London Gazette (or equivalents in other countries)

It is necessary to be familiar with the legal structure of debtor companies and also to be aware of their links with other companies and past events.

In the UK, this information is recorded in the London Gazette, which is a highly specialised publication that caters to the public, private and voluntary sectors. Corporate insolvency and personal bankruptcies are recorded, as are the appointment of administrators and liquidators, the meetings of creditors, petitions and orders to wind up companies, etc. This is extremely useful information to credit insurers. In addition, information companies, such as Experian, are also used for reporting insolvencies.

The possible links with past events can be particularly important. Perhaps the director of a new company was recently involved in the insolvency of another company (experience has shown that some people are just chronically incapable of running a company, but persist in starting new ones, time after time). Others may have a reputation for 'organised' insolvencies, using practices that are almost criminal.

Annual accounts

It is indisputable that the use of up-to-date financial information is the most crucial weapon in the credit insurer's risk analysis arsenal. The prime source of this information is the company's annual accounts. European law states that incorporated companies are legally obliged to file their accounts with registrars in the country in which they are registered. These accounts must be made available to the public domain. From a credit insurance point of view, we would prefer to see fully *audited* accounts.

At one time, it was thought that 'non-profit organisations' (such as charities, political associations, hospitals or churches) should fall outside the operational sphere of credit insurers. More recent experience has shown that this was a mistaken belief. Such organisations often engage in commercial activity (at the very least, with the idea that any profit made can be re-invested back into the organisation, which, of course, trades in its own right). Although there is a perception that the risk level is lower in this sector, in the UK a NHS trust (hospital) was placed in administration in 2012 and even schools can now be forced to close.

FOOD FOR THOUGHT

In Europe, the majority of companies qualify to be considered as micro-companies. As a result of new European legislation, in future there will be much less publicly available information in respect of these companies. This will make the task of the supplier and the credit insurer much harder.

In Germany, the credit insurers have already had bitter experience of what the non-filing of this kind of financial information can entail. Until recently, only stock-listed companies were required to publish their annual accounts. This made risk calculation in Europe's largest economy something of a hit-and-miss affair. Fortunately, this position was changed by a new law that came into effect on 1 January 2007.

a) Traditional financial analysis

The traditional method of reviewing the financial performance and stability of a company is to review its balance sheet, looking in particular at certain key ratios and parameters:

- The net assets of a company available to equity shareholders, which is equivalent to the total equity of the company after deducting non-tangible fixed assets. (In other words, this means deducting intangible assets that have been capitalised, such as acquisition brands, IPR, goodwill, etc.)

- Solvency ratio (equity capital as a proportion of the total balance sheet). Generally, the higher the percentage, the more stable the company
- Liquidity ratio (calculated as the ratio of current assets on the balance sheet to current liabilities).

The profit and loss account. Operating profit is calculated by looking at earnings before interest and tax, discounting any extraordinary income and expenditure. Credit insurers are particularly interested in the figures for operating profit (before the deduction of financial and other extraordinary budgetary postings).

b) International financial reporting standards (IFRS)

Since 1 January 2005, stock-listed companies have been obliged to draw up their annual accounts in accordance with the IFRS norms. The aim was to standardise financial reporting, so that the differences between countries could be eliminated in the interests of greater efficiency and transparency.

The core idea is that the company's tangible assets must be valued at their fair value and that on this basis the company must regularly carry out an impairment test. This same principle also applies to non-tangible assets, such as goodwill. Correct valuation lies at the very heart of financial reporting. Until recently, most annual accounts in Europe were prepared on the basis of the depreciated (sunk) cost price, so that the assets were seriously undervalued. Fortunately, this is no longer acceptable in the current complex economic world.

IFRS also obliges companies to produce a cash-flow statement. This is a practice that was already common in the Anglo-Saxon world, but was not compulsory in terms of the accounting norms applicable in other countries (such as Belgium). A cash-flow statement provides the analyst with much useful data, since it allows the company's liquidity, as expressed in its changing cash position, to be followed and monitored. This is the real cash-flow and reflects a short-term perspective – the vision that is the most important from the credit insurer's point of view. It allows him to assess whether the company, on the basis of its anticipated operations and after investments, will generate sufficient liquid resources to honour its outstanding financial obligations (principal repayments and interest). In other words, it goes a long way towards establishing the company's repayment ability.

→ *The management and the shareholders*

Assessing the quality of the management and the shareholders is a subjective matter, but should nonetheless not be overlooked. In this respect, the experience of the credit insurer's analyst is key. Is the management competent (are there no negative reports recorded in the database) and do they have the support of the shareholders (what decisions were taken at the last AGM)? The code of practice of the managers is also important: have they been involved in a previous corporate or other insolvency and, if so, how did they react?

ATTENTION!

In recent years there has been a noticeable decline in operational ethics in the business world. Past experience shows that many groups no longer hesitate to allow their (mostly overseas) subsidiaries to fail, once they realise that the necessary restructuring costs have become too great. This pattern is regrettable – and makes the credit insurer's task much more difficult.

→ *Relations with customers and suppliers*

How good is the relationship of the debtor with his customers and suppliers? Is the customer portfolio sufficiently diversified, or is it concentrated on just a few large names? In this latter instance, the risk is much greater: the loss of one of these key customers could lead to a huge fall in turnover, which may no longer be adequate to cover the company's fixed costs. Here insolvency becomes much more probable – as past experience has proven time and time again.

→ *Age of the company*

GOOD TO KNOW

Within the context of a scarcity of financial information, the age of the company is also relevant. Statistics show that young companies are more likely to fail, particularly during their first years of trading.

In the UK, the following recent statistics (2013) chart the default probabilities for companies with no accounts. No distinction has been made between unlimited or limited companies.

TABLE 5.1: *Default probabilities for companies with no accounts (source: Euler Hermes)*

Company age (years)	Definition of company	Default probability
0 –2	Start-up	0.34%
2 – 4	New	0.52%
4 – 6	New to Established	0.22%
6 – 8	Established	0.17%
8 – 14	Established to Old	0.16%
+ 14	Old	0.14%

We can see that companies between 2 and 4 years old have the highest risk of default and that this default probability decreases with the age of the company. In response to this large number of failures amongst start-up businesses, the legislators in various countries have introduced the concept of founder's liability. All too frequently in the past, companies were founded without sufficient capital to make the initial investments that were necessary to make them viable. Some even went insolvent before their official registration was completed!

→ *Payment record*

The payment record of the debtor is one of the most vital of all signals for the credit insurer. A debtor with liquidity problems will first settle his commitments with the banks (his credit line) and the government (tax and social insurance). Next, he will appeal to his suppliers for leniency, starting with those with whom he has had the longest commercial relationship. The aim is to secure a temporary deferment of payment for his outstanding invoices. A supplier who is covered for credit insurance may be willing to grant this request, but must inform his credit insurer in advance. Failure to do so is a breach of the policy conditions.

WHAT YOU SHOULD REALLY KNOW

If a number of insured customers notify a request for deferment of payment by the same buyer/debtor, this provides the credit insurer with information of great value. Thanks to the introduction in recent years of a worldwide business model by the large international credit insurance groups, this key warning signal has gained even more significance.

→ *Structured warning signals*

Credit insurers also receive other negative information in a structured form via bulk loading or web-services. Warning signals are particularly important for sole traders, since the insurer does not usually have detailed information about these debtors at his disposal (because they are not required to file accounts with the national authority). These warning signals include:

- overdue payments to the tax and/or social insurance authorities; statistically, this latter default has a huge predictive value;
- summons issued by social insurance and other social security institutions in various sectors;
- officially submitted protests against unredeemed bills of exchange (although this has diminished in both number and importance in recent years);
- the evolution of the Paydex (payment index), as made available by the various commercial information agencies;
- postponement of the official publication of the annual account (normally 9 months after the closure of the financial year); this can indicate that the company in question has something to hide;
- termination of a company VAT number or repeated inspection visits by the VAT authorities;
- past association (of individuals) with negative events (administration, CVA, liquidation and the winding-up of companies).

→ *Other negative information*

In the UK, Experian or other credit agencies are used to seek information about whether companies have county court judgments (CCJs) pending against them. This information is not recorded at Companies House. Experian receive this information from the Registered Trust Central Organisation.

Other items of negative information that can be of importance to the credit insurer include:

- the previously unexpected reduction or termination of credit limits, especially before the anticipated expiry date;
- the existence of previous arrears, claim submissions, loss compensation payments, etc. in respect of specific debtors;
- negative details obtained from other third party sources, such as the press, sector contacts, company visits, etc.

CHAPTER 6
RATINGS

A rating is an estimate of the creditworthiness of the subject being assessed: this can be a company, a country or even a sector. Historically, ratings agencies grew up in the USA, to provide the banks and the investment community generally with a simple guide to the financial strength of an investment opportunity. Good risks became known as 'investment grade' and bad ones as 'junk'. Investment grade risks, in turn, paid far less for their borrowings than others. Ratings in modern times have become much more common across the world, to the extent that most significant businesses now seek to develop one for themselves. Unfortunately, far too many banks and lenders became complacent, neglected to apply their own analysis models and fell into almost complete dependence on the ratings agencies. The financial crash of 2008-2009 was in no small measure due to banks failing to do their own analysis on risks, about which they understood little.

WHAT YOU NEED TO KNOW

The creation of ratings plays a central role in the credit insurer's preventative task, allowing him as far as reasonably possible to separate the healthy companies from the unhealthy ones. For this task, the credit insurer has designed his own risk analysis model, which is in no way dependent on outside ratings agencies. It is essential, therefore, that this rating system is as accurate and reliable as possible.

In this chapter we will explain the most important rating principles. Although we will briefly say something about other ratings (sector and country), we will concentrate most of our attention on corporate businesses. We will also explain why ratings are now considered crucial for a credit insurer. As an example, we will look at the credit rating system used by Euler Hermes, since this is the system about which we are best informed.

As far as terminology is concerned, it is perhaps worth noting that the word 'grading' is sometimes used in credit insurance circles instead of 'rating'. In general, however, 'rating' is more common in an international context, and so we will continue to use that term.

1 General

1.1 TYPES OF RATING

Credit insurers distinguish three different types of rating:

1. Company ratings: As described above, in the past the calculation and issue of ratings was the preserve of recognised rating bureaux, such as Standard & Poor's Ratings Services, Moody's Investors Service or Fitch Ratings, who provided ratings for companies on request, primarily for use by the investment community. A.M. Best grew up by specialising (as it continues to do to this day) in rating the insurance industry. In light of Basel II (the second round of regulatory edicts concerned with the assessment of capital charges in relation to counter-party or credit risk taken by commercial banks), most banks have now developed their own internal rating systems. Credit insurers also recognised the importance of developing their own models during the 1990's. The commercial information agencies, such as Graydon or Dun & Bradstreet, were also quick to follow.
2. Country ratings: Once again, there are numerous sources: inter-governmental agencies, rating bureaux (Standard & Poor's, Moody's and Fitch), commercial banks, commercial information agencies (particularly Dun & Bradstreet, with its worldwide presence), magazines (Institutional Investor, Euromoney, Economic Intelligence Unit) and – last but not least – the credit insurers.
3. Sector ratings: There are various institutions occupied with this aspect of rating, but their number is fewer. Some credit insurers also give sector ratings.

The company rating is the result of a micro-economic analysis and primarily assesses commercial risk. The country rating is the result of a macro-economic analysis, including possible political risks.

GOOD TO KNOW

It is not easy to obtain accurate and detailed information about rating models; most rating institutions regard their rating system and the manner in which it operates as a matter of the greatest secrecy, since it is the very foundation of their activities and the key element in their competitive strategy. Since 2008-2009, however, industry regulators have been seeking to monitor these systems.

Already, government authorities are increasingly insistent on more openness in matters relating to rating calculation. The old Basel II regulations stipulated three broad methods for calculating capital charges for credit risk:

1 A standardised approach (the successor to the 1988 Basel I accord, with some additional risk sensitivity) based on the use of a wider range of risk weights, linked to external ratings.
2 A basic, internal-ratings approach, whereby the financial institution splits its risk portfolio into broad categories of exposure and then assigns ratings, linked to probability of default. Other inputs are set by the relevant banking supervisor.
3 An advanced internal-ratings approach, whereby the financial institution adds to the results of the previous approach its own estimates of loss for any default, as well as its probable exposure to that default.

As can be seen, rating is a key element in this policy. Giving credit to a company with a good rating makes a much lower demand on the bank's own capital resources. Unfortunately, the financial and economic crisis of 2008-2009 demonstrated that the then existing mechanisms were not adequate enough to prevent disaster, so that Basel III is currently in preparation.

The credit insurance sector will soon be subject to a similar set of monitoring controls, when Solvency II comes into effect. Originally destined to become law in 2013, the whole drafting process now seems (at the present time of writing) to be heading back to the drawing board, since a number of the proposals have not been deemed fit for purpose (for example, the initial draft suggested that insurance companies, including pension funds, would no longer be able to invest in commercial banks). It is now expected that Solvency II will come into effect at the start of 2016.

1.2 SOVEREIGN CEILING

It is self-evident that a credit insurer uses the three different types of rating in a complementary way. When he is asked to give an opinion about a company that operates in a particular sector in a particular country, it is the totality of the risk that he must assess: assessing one or other of the three elements on a stand-alone basis is not acceptable. As a general rule, the country rating is more important than the sector rating and the individual company rating. This is referred to as the sovereign ceiling.

1.3 VALIDITY OF A RATING: ONE YEAR

The ratings from private credit insurers normally remain valid for a period of one year, following which they must be revised and updated.

This is, of course, related to the fact that credit insurance is exclusively concerned with commercial credit provision in the short term.

The rating reflects the risk-likelihood of a company becoming insolvent in the following 12 months.

1.4 DIFFERENT METHODOLOGIES

We have already mentioned the different institutions and organisations that publish ratings, each with a different method of calculation.

ATTENTION!

Although all these rating systems essentially serve the same purpose (i.e. to establish a level of creditworthiness), the use of different methodologies leads to different classifications, based on different terminologies. This makes it difficult to compare the systems. For this reason, it is important in each case to look closely at what the ratings really mean.

In this chapter, we will confine ourselves to the methodology of the credit insurance sector and, in particular, the Euler Hermes system.

2 Company ratings

We will first describe the general context and the principles, on the basis of which ratings are generated either via an automated system (with the help, amongst other things, of statistical scoring) or manually.

2.1 DEFINITION

A rating is a method of measuring and indicating the level of solvency of a debtor, based on different criteria that estimate the repayment ability of a company over a particular period of time. This period is one year for credit insurers (short term) and five years for the capital market (long term).

A rating from a credit insurer is therefore an expression of the intrinsic trade credit risk associated with a debtor, the risk in question being the likelihood of insolvency. The rating is only a synthetic indicator of the company's creditworthiness. An investor who, for example, is thinking of buying shares in a company must also refer to ratings that relate specifically to investment risk. The importance of the rating is that it provides a simple indicator, which compresses what would otherwise be an enormous amount of financial risk information.

2.2 CATEGORIES OF COMPANY RATINGS

Credit insurers distinguish between two different types of company ratings: individual ratings and group ratings.

→ *Individual ratings*

Every company is allocated an individual rating on the basis of specific criteria.

→ *Group ratings*

This is the rating for groups of companies (multinational or not). Various individual companies can belong to a group. This implies that they are in some way linked to each other; for example, through common shareholders. Within the context of an increasingly globalised world economy, this is becoming more and more common. It is perfectly possible for an international group to have a good credit rating, while one of its local branches or subsidiaries has a poor rating at national level. The fact that the 'weak' local company is part of a 'strong' international group is certainly a factor that needs to be taken into account in the financial analysis. It is for this reason that some financial institutions, including the credit insurers, prefer to give a rating for the multinational group.

GOOD TO KNOW

If in the past a group has shown itself willing to support its weak local subsidiaries in difficult times, this can help to bolster the individual ratings of the local subsidiaries in question. In some cases, it can even bring their rating up to the level of the group as a whole. This is known as a grade transfer.

However, it is important to bear the following comments in mind:

1 Such group ratings are always calculated manually.
2 The standard of behaviour shown by the group in the past is a particularly important factor. Such are the complexities of current trading patterns that groups are sometimes given little choice but to allow weak subsidiaries to be declared insolvent, in order to ensure the survival of the rest of the group. The biggest victims of this trend are the suppliers – a fact that can have a strong negative influence on the group rating.

2.3 RATING CHARACTERISTICS FOR CREDIT INSURANCE

→ ***Unsolicited ratings***

The large rating agencies, such as Standard & Poor's, Moody's, Fitch and A.M. Best, usually give ratings on request (solicited ratings); for example, when a company wants to issue new bonds in the public financial market. This is accompanied by a thorough auditing of the company in question. The better the rating, the cheaper the premium for launching a new issue will be. (Incidentally, credit insurers should not be confused with bond insurers, who, historically, insured or 'securitised' bond issues to investors. This was very popular in the United States with the monoliners (such as Ambac), who originally only covered low risk municipal bonds, but gradually insured CDOs and other derivatives. For this reason, several such agencies failed to survive the financial crash of 2008-2009).

In recent times, the rating bureaux have come in for increasing criticism for the ratings they applied to bundled risks (for example, where mortgage companies bundled up huge numbers of outstanding loans, as security for a new bond issue). They were also deemed to be guilty of waiting far too long to downgrade certain companies and countries. This was the case with the East Asian 'tiger' economies in 1997, with Enron in 2001 and more recently in 2006-2007, with the structured financial products offered by many banks, which led first to the sub-prime credit crisis and then to the major financial collapse of 2008.

In theory, credit insurers give unsolicited ratings, in the sense that the ratings are not requested by the debtors to whom they apply. Instead, they are notified to the policyholder (supplier). In this way, ratings become part of the default management policy of the insurers and their policyholders. This type of rating is usually based on less information, since in most cases the insurer can only base his assessment on proprietary information or data that is available in the public domain. As a result, unsolicited ratings tend to be lower than solicited ones and more conservative in the evaluation of the company.

USEFUL TIP

Some people regard unsolicited ratings as more objective than solicited ratings, since they are not influenced by the informal relationship that might have built up over the years between the rating agency and the companies they review.

→ *Point-in-time (PIT)*

Credit insurers apply a point-in-time philosophy. Their rating systems evaluate the creditworthiness of a company in the short term on the basis of the most recent available information. As a result, the ratings are more ephemeral and more dependent on macro-economic developments. During a recession, the ratings of the agencies will fall and during a boom they will improve. However, International Credit Insurance & Surety Association (ICISA) data shows that global exposure has returned to 2008 levels (circa 1,800 billion euros), notwithstanding the ongoing fiscal malaise and the slow return to growth in the developed world.

The alternative to PIT is known as the through-the-cycle philosophy (TTC). These rating systems calculate the average failure risk over a period covering one or more economic cycles. This means that the agency ratings are relatively stable over a number of years and do not correlate with the short-term ups and downs of the economy. This is the philosophy used, for example, by Standard and Poor's to estimate the financial resilience of companies in the long term.

2.4 HOW A RATING IS CREATED

There are two main methods for the calculation of a rating: the automatic rating (without any manual intervention) and the manual rating (based on a detailed study carried out by a credit analyst).

→ *Automatic ratings*

A rating is automatically allocated to a company on the basis of one of two automated techniques:

1. A statistical technique, known as scoring. On the basis of a predetermined model, each company is given its own score. The value range in which this score falls determines the corresponding rating category of the company. The fact that in most European and North American countries the majority of companies are obliged to officially declare and file their annual accounts makes it possible to develop a good scoring model, since there is a relative wealth of structured information.
2. An expert system, when sufficient structured information is lacking. This is the system used in general by Euler Hermes for sole traders. In this instance a 'fuzzy logic' algorithm is applied, which is based on the experience of experts over many years.

An expert system offers the following advantages:
- It requires relatively little historical data.
- It is possible to make use of your own experts, which allows the results to be more easily accepted in-house.
- It is a flexible system that can be adjusted quickly and easily, as market circumstances dictate.

Unfortunately, there are also a number of disadvantages:
- The acquisition of the necessary knowledge and experience can take a great deal of time, often a number of years.
- The quality of the model is wholly dependent on the quality of the experts.

The main advantage of the automated scoring system is that the subjective element, which inevitably attaches to the opinion of an expert, is removed. Automatic systems produce ratings on a continuous basis and in a standardised manner. This also means that many more companies can be given a rating than with the time-consuming manual method, which therefore increases both productivity and efficiency.

ATTENTION!

There are two disadvantages with an automated rating. The first is that automated calculations usually have a margin of error. Although there are control mechanisms to ensure that the deviations remain within limits, it is never possible to exclude the possibility of a mistake. The second is that a manual rating can 'disagree' with the auto-decision, so that consistency is lost.

→ *Manual ratings*

These are not necessarily an alternative to automated ratings – the two systems often work hand-in-glove. This helps to smooth work flows and allows manual decisions to focus on the most difficult cases.

A manual rating is created by a credit analyst, who will investigate the company in depth and assign a rating from his own assessment. The criteria he uses to grade a risk are based on four categories: Ownership, Management & Strategy; Revenue & Profitability; Liquidity & Financial Leverage; Cash Flow & Coverage.

If any previous unethical behaviour (willful non-payment, etc.) is uncovered, a harsh view will be taken. This is particularly the case for 'phoenix' companies. (A phoenix company is a commercial entity which has emerged from the collapse of another company through insolvency. The new company is set up to conduct the same or similar trading activities as the former, and is able to present the appearance of 'business as usual' to its customers. The purchase of the insolvent company's assets occurs in general at a knock-down pace). This harsh judgement is not only applied to multinational groups who have previously left their creditors in the lurch by allowing subsidiaries to flounder, but is also relevant on a wider basis.

If there is evidence of group support, a similar core activity, the same name, etc., the grade will be shared across the group. Separate criteria also exist to examine multinational groups and subsidiaries.

The criteria applicable for the setting of individual company ratings are broadly the same as those used for the calculation of group ratings.

> **GOOD TO KNOW**
>
> A manual calculation is generally used for companies with a large outstanding risk or for debtors in difficulties. These are known as sensitive risks, and warrant the more detailed, case-specific manual approach.

Nevertheless, a manual analysis remains in essence subjective, so that (small) differences between different analysts are possible. The most important thing is the future of the company: for this reason, more attention should be focused on the qualitative elements (management, strategy, etc.) and less on the quantitative elements (financial data). The latter only shows the performance of the company in the recent past; in other words, it looks backwards and not forwards.

2.5 THE RATINGS USED BY INTERNATIONAL CREDIT INSURERS (EULER HERMES)

It is not easy for an international credit insurance group to develop a uniform system:

- → Countries do not all have the same quantity of relevant information or the same method of structuring it.
- → The definitions of default and insolvency are also different in different countries. Some countries have relatively few official insolvencies (such as Spain, for example). This is linked to differences in culture, but also to the applicable legislation of the country concerned. In this respect, there is still no uniformity throughout the European Union.

Even so, it is important for the international groups that everyone gives a rating to debtors that can be interpreted in the same manner everywhere.

TABLE 6.1 *Rating classifications in the Euler Hermes group (source: Euler Hermes)*

Euler Hermes Grade	Rating Standard & Poor's	Risk definition
1	AAA AA–	outstanding
2	AA– A–	strong
3	A– BBB	good
4	BBB BBB–	above average
5	BBB– BB–	average
6	BB– B	below average
7	CCC+ CCC–	weak
8	CCC– C	high risk
9	C D	uninsurable
10	Not applicable	insolvent

→ *Rating classifications*

Euler Hermes identifies ten different rating classifications that it uses for all its business ratings (both automated and manual). Grade 1 contains the companies with an excellent level of creditworthiness. Grade 10 contains the companies that are commercially 'dead in the water' (i.e. are subject to any form of administration, official insolvency, liquidation, termination of business activities, etc.).

Table 6.1 shows the different classifications, together with the ratings used by Standard and Poor's. It must be emphasised that this comparison is purely illustrative, since the ratings themselves differ fundamentally: Euler Hermes estimates the likelihood of insolvency and the probability of default over a period of just one year, whereas the Standard and Poor's rating looks at the same likelihood over a much longer period.

Euler Hermes Grade 5 marks the limit of investment grade risk. Companies with a lower rating are not such good risks. From Grade 7, Euler Hermes speaks of sensitive (i.e. bad) risks. Nevertheless, an experienced underwriter may still offer insurance cover on a sensitive risk grade, providing there are good enough reasons to justify the decision.

GOOD TO KNOW

The ratings must convey the same message of creditworthiness. To make this possible, international groups make use of what is known as 'failure rates'.

→ *Failure rates (probability of default)*

To understand the concept of failure rates, it is first necessary to give a definition of a default as applied in credit insurance, and afterwards to examine the mechanisms of the official insolvency (failure) rate.

a ***What is a default?***
Failure of the buyer to pay what he owes is at the heart of the credit insurer's business. This sounds simple enough. But an understanding of what the financial incapacity of a buyer actually means is much more complicated.

The credit insurer must make a forward projection to take into account the likely ability to meet future commitments. This can be either positive or negative. As a positive example, larger than standard amounts of cover were underwritten in the run-up to the 2012 London Olympics, on the basis of the secure nature of the contracts with the end user. As a negative example, a company may have shown that it has the ability and the funds to pay their short term debts, but an underwriter may be aware that the outside environment is changing for the worse. The end of feed-in tariffs for the renewable energy companies in the UK is a good example of this.

A buyer therefore 'fails' when he fails to settle his debts. This may involve simple non-payment and not necessarily a formal declaration of insolvency. The credit insurer's protracted default cover becomes applicable in these circumstances. The period defined by protracted default varies from market to market and in accordance with the agreed terms of payment and maximum extension period (MEP), as detailed in the individual policy. The protracted default period starts at the end of the MEP (typically 60 days after the due date) and runs for 90 days in AA (UK where even 60 days is possible, Western EU, USA, etc.) rated markets, for 180 days in BB (Poland, Mexico, etc.) and B (India, China) rated markets, 270 days for C markets (Romania, Egypt) and 360 days for

D markets (Argentina, Serbia). Claims are settled at the end of the protracted default period specified for the market in question.

b ***Definition of a failure rate***

The ideal point of reference to allow the different rating systems within an international group to be compared with each other is the likelihood of failure, usually referred to as the probability of default or, more simply, the failure rate. Because the different rating systems in different countries are built up in a different manner, Euler Hermes has developed different types of failure rates, which make it possible to compare these systems on several criteria. The most common type of failure rate, and the easiest to calculate, is the official insolvency rate, based on the number of official insolvencies.

The failure rate for a particular rating class is obtained by taking the total number of companies that fail in that classification during a particular year (the observation period) and comparing this figure as a proportion of the total number of companies in that class at the beginning of the observation period. In this way, the failure rate estimates the probability that a company in that class will fail in the year ahead (probability of default). For this reason, failure rates must never be more than one year old. For example, on 1 March in year X (observation date) there are 1,000 companies in rating class 7. During the following year, up to and including 28 February in year X+1, (observation period), 100 of these companies fail. The failure rate for class 7 is therefore 10%.

c ***Official insolvency rate***

As mentioned above, the official insolvency rate is the most common type of failure rate. It is based on the actual occurrence of official insolvency in each country. (In the UK, the Department of Business Innovation and Skills releases quarterly data on insolvency proceedings issued at county court level in England & Wales. The Insolvency Service publishes parallel data.)

The definition of the rate is as follows:

$$\frac{\text{The number of companies declared insolvent by the courts during the observation period}}{\text{The total number of companies with a rating on the observation date}}$$

Using this definition, the official insolvency rate – the likelihood that a company will become insolvent during the next 12 months – can be calculated for each individual rating class. This broad definition can then be broken down further, to provide an analysis of possible failures within individual trade sectors (for example, what is the likelihood of a grade 6 company failing in the retail sector compared with the pharmaceutical sector?).

→ *Automatic limit decisions*

In today's world of credit insurance, efficiency and automation are of crucial importance. For this reason, most credit insurers now link the ratings of companies to an automatic limit decision. This means that whenever an application for a credit limit for a company is received by the insurer online, the system first checks to see whether or not such an automatic decision limit already exists. An underwriter contacted by telephone would also check this. There are four possible outcomes:

1. The limit exists and is sufficient. The application is automatically approved.
2. The limit exists but is insufficient. The application is provisionally approved up to the level of the limit, with the balance being passed on to an underwriter for manual processing.
3. There is no automatic limit. The application is referred for a manual check, where the limit is assessed by the individual underwriter.
4. The auto-model is set to 'risk refusal'. The application is declined and a nil limit is issued.

2.6 THE ADDED VALUE OF A RATING WITH A CREDIT INSURER

The rating creates a number of other possibilities for the credit insurer. In particular, the grading can be considered as core to the management of existing risks.

→ *Increasing operational efficiency*

Within the framework of the credit insurer's prevention policy, credit monitoring plays a key role. This can be done much more efficiently if the companies have a rating, since the attention of monitoring staff can be focused on the debtors with a lower rating and a higher global outstanding risk. At Euler Hermes, for example, insured debtors are given an internal review category ranging from 0 to 3 depending on their grade number and the amount of cover endorsed, where 0 = no active monitoring and 3 = proactive monitoring by a local credit analyst.

Companies with a good rating are generally monitored less stringently, although well-graded buyers with large exposures are still actively checked. A special risk team exists within Euler Hermes specifically for this purpose, and is considered key to this ongoing activity. In general, however, time and energy are invested in the cases that are likely to yield the most important benefits from the point of view of managing credit risk.

As mentioned previously, the rating can be linked to an automatic limit decision, so that relatively minor credit applications can be approved directly online, without the necessity for any manual intervention.

→ ***Price-setting is not definitive, but is linked to the risk profile of the debt portfolio.***

Prices are generally set on the basis of estimated insurable turnover notified at the moment of inception or renewal. This turnover is assessed together with the trade sector, loss history and policy structure to form the pricing. The risk portfolio obviously forms a significant part of this calculation.

In credit insurance the rating is the basis for considerable statistical research and investigation. Principally, it assists in the calculation of the probability of default for each rating class (based on past experience). The analysis is made for the entire risk portfolio, and is carried out by the credit insurer's local offices in every country where it operates (since each country has its own specific risk characteristics).

The probability of default and other statistical risk factors (for example, the use factor of the granted nominal limits: see chapter 4) therefore offer the credit insurer the possibility to calculate the premium for the insured party with greater accuracy, in accordance with the risk profile of his debt portfolio and its expected loss. This is now feasible, because in principle every company has an internal rating.

GOOD TO KNOW

In this way, indirect account is also taken of the principle of mutualisation within the risk portfolio. A credit insurer wants to see a spread of risk and a range of grades.

→ ***Increasing commercial competitiveness***

Insured parties receive a superior service, both in terms of speed and quality, through the more efficient organisation of internal processes. One example of this is the 'proactive' decision. When the limit on a debtor has previously been restricted (for example, an application was made for £100,000 but a limit of

£50,000 approved), rejected or terminated, the subsequent upgrading of the debtor's case file, following receipt of new and more positive information, will prompt the insurer to inform the insured customer that a new credit application would now be approved.

Moreover, the rating also makes it possible to develop various new products and services that can provide the credit insurer with additional fee business. Euler Hermes, for example, now sells 'credit intelligence opinions' to insured clients for cover under their discretionary limit. With its new 'Simplicity' product (aimed at SME's), a policyholder can increase his indemnity from a standard 60% to 90%, by applying for a grade on a specific customer. This will be agreed if the customer is graded 1 to 6; the indemnity remains at 60% if the customer is graded 7; and cover is refused for grades 8 to 10.

→ *Consistent credit policy within a worldwide group*

Within a multinational group, created through the take-over and merging of different national units, it is not easy to create a common culture. We have already seen in table 2.2 (payment behaviour in Europe) that there are huge differences in attitudes and opinions between Northern Europe and Southern Europe. Similar differences also exist with regard to risk perception.

When the various national units of the credit insurer issue a credit rating, it is important that they should place debtors with a similar credit risk in the same rating class. In other words, comparable debtors in different countries must be given the same rating. This can be checked on the basis of the failure rate (probability of default): this must be approximately the same for each rating class in each local branch office. Even so, absolute parity is not always feasible, since each local market has its own specific characteristics.

GOOD TO KNOW

Every rating is linked to a specific credit policy, whether a 'live' policy or a prospective new contract. This assessment and the resulting action must be the same for every local office within the credit insurance group. For example, when a buyer receives a 9 rating from Euler Hermes, it is always the intention, wherever the company operates, to reduce the potential of the default risk as quickly as possible, since the insolvency of the debtor is highly likely to follow.

→ *Reinsurance policy*

Reinsurance is insurance for insurance companies. It allows direct insurers to spread the risks they underwrite amongst other (specialist) risk-carriers. Reinsurance provides 'surrogate', or 'hybrid', or 'synthetic' capital. Effectively, the function of credit reinsurance is the provision of additional risk capital for the credit insurance company, which allows it to achieve several different objectives:

- By sharing risk with others, the credit insurer lowers his own capitals exposure when losses occur.
- By purchasing capacity, he can underwrite larger amounts of risk than his own capital would have allowed.
- By being able to take on larger amounts of risk, he increases his premium-earning capability.
- By laying off 'peaks' of larger risks, he can create a better balance and spread of risks within his portfolio.
- By laying off risk to others, he needs less premium reserves.
- By using reinsurance as a financial management tool, he can reduce volatility in the company's bottom-line results, earnings stream and share price.

Reinsurance is about laying off (ceding) risks to either a single reinsurance company or a series of them. Normally, before the credit insurer underwrites risks, he will have entered into a framework agreement (known as a reinsurance treaty) with the reinsurance company/companies, detailing how the risk-ceding process will work.

Reinsurers obviously need to understand how the credit insurer's risk management system operates and will also need to understand how the credit insurer's risk models work in detail.

The reinsurance options for the credit insurer (and the related costs) are determined to a large extent by the risk profile of the global credit insurance portfolio (as expressed through the totality of the different company, trade sector and country ratings).

→ ***Rating of the credit insurer***

WHAT YOU NEED TO KNOW

The credit insurer's own rating is of crucial importance to the insured party. The insured party has arranged a policy with the insurer to provide him with cover that will pay him compensation for loss in the event of the default of one or more of his debtors. When the debt is not settled on the date due for payment, he has the right to submit a compensation claim – but he also needs to know that he can reasonably expect the insurer to pay this claim in full and on time! He has enough problems with the creditworthiness of his debtors: he doesn't need to also worry about the creditworthiness of his insurer!

In March 2012, all the major credit insurance groups had strong credit ratings (see their respective websites). Their long-term ratings were as follows:

- Euler Hermes: Standard & Poor's: AA- (August 2012, outlook stable)
- Atradius: Standard & Poor's: BBB (October 2012, outlook negative); A.M. Best: A (September 2012, outlook stable); Moody's: A3 (October 2012, outlook negative)
- Coface: Fitch: AA- (May 2012, outlook stable); Moody's: A2 (December 2012, outlook stable)

3 Sector ratings

Before moving on, we will first look briefly at sector ratings, which are often less discussed than the 'more important' company and country ratings. Even so, it should be obvious that the analysis of a sector in a particular region can be of crucial value to a credit insurer when assessing default risks.

This being said, not everyone in the credit insurance sector monitors this useful marker. Euler Hermes, Atradius and Coface are the only groups that make their sector studies publicly available. In these studies, each sector in each country is given an aggregate rating.

4 Country ratings (Euler Hermes)

4.1 GENERAL

In contrast to the company ratings, country ratings are largely based on macro-economic indicators. Country risk can be defined as 'the systemic conditions and events that are beyond the control of individual actors (companies, government authorities and private citizens) and can lead to payment default'.

We will examine the country ratings as used by the Euler Hermes private credit insurance group. In short, they are a combination of the estimated economic and political risks of the country in question. The perspective is still short term (maximum of one year).

> **ATTENTION!**
>
> We need to be clear that we are discussing the credit ratings of the private credit insurer Euler Hermes and not the ratings of Hermes, a public credit insurer that acts for the German state and is also part of the Euler Hermes group. The country ratings of the latter are based on the OECD classification (as is the case for all other public credit insurers).

4.2 THE ECONOMIC RISK

This risk is determined by two factors that can have an impact on systemic economic risk:

1. Macro-economic imbalances. These can give rise to one or more 'events', such as devaluation of the currency, a sharp fall in GDP, a shortage of foreign currency or even bank crises.

   The basis of this part of the risk analysis is a scoring system that consists of 30 structured macro-economic indicators. These indicators include: real domestic credit growth and inflation; growth in GDP; level of budget surplus/shortfall; foreign or public debt in relation to GDP; arrears of payment in respect of global foreign debt; current account balance (liquid reserves); level of imports covered by foreign currency reserves; short-term debt and the repayment pattern of long-term debt in relation to monetary reserves; the health of the banking system. The purpose is to investigate the health of the economic structure and its relation to fiscal and monetary policy.

The indicators deal with quantitative variables. The resulting score gives an indication of the economic rating of the country, but the analyst can adjust this rating if he feels that he has sufficiently valid reasons to do so. The score therefore supports rather than determines the analysis.

2 The institutional/structural factors present in the business environment. These factors show whether flourishing companies are encouraged or discouraged. Once again, a series of 30 variables is used for this part of the analysis, which are either quantitative or involve perception indices. These variables are supplemented by standardised information sources (such as the World Bank's study entitled *Ease of Doing Business*), which make comparisons between countries possible.

GOOD TO KNOW

Although not all variables are easy to quantify, Euler Hermes has developed its own Structural Business Environment Model. This examines factors such as infrastructure, bureaucracy and regulation, corruption (the Corruption Perception Index compiled by Transparency International), respect for property rights and due process of law, human development, openness, a positive government approach to business, the banking system, corporate governance, etc.

4.3 THE POLITICAL RISK

The political risks covered are inconvertibility of exchange, contract frustration, (for example, by civil war), contract cancellation, import and export restrictions, etc. Unless the buyer is an arm of an overseas government, these causes of loss need to be established as being beyond the control of either seller or buyer.

The political risk rating is based on two separate elements:

1 Possible systemic political weakness. This can be identified, for example, by a lack of clear procedures for the appointment of new governments, excessive concentrations of power, a lack of institutional freedom, direct governmental interference in the economy (e.g. foreign currency restrictions), social division, etc. These can all lead to the disruption of economic performance.

2 Ineffective governments. This relates to political weaknesses that limit the ability of the government to react effectively in times of crisis.

4.4 THE COMBINATION: ECONOMIC RISK + POLITICAL RISK = COUNTRY RATING

At Euler Hermes the combination of economic risk and political risk will result in a country being awarded one of six country ratings: the best is AA (for example, the United States and most countries in the European Union); D is the weakest. From the rating BB downwards, countries start to display weaknesses in their economic structure, in the implementation of economic policy, and in their ability to withstand economic and political shocks on a local, regional and global basis. The country rating is, above all, a reflection of the transfer and convertibility risk.

4.5 THE IMPORTANCE OF A COUNTRY RATING

GOOD TO KNOW

The country rating is of great importance for a credit insurer. In principle, it is the first rating to be applied, taking precedence over both sector and company ratings. A high risk country rating increases the risk profile of a debtor and will therefore also have an effect on the calculation of premium.

Credit insurers generally devise a credit policy that is linked through their procedures to the rating of a country. The elements that can vary on the basis of the country rating when credit limits are being set include:
- maximum payment period;
- an open account basis (this is the least secure way to do business; there are no guarantees for the seller) or irrevocable documentary credits;
- maximum period for payment deferment/extension;
- level of discretionary limits;
- acceptance of binding contracts;
- cover percentage (in principle, 90%);
- claims waiting period: this is the period of time that an insured party must wait after the submission of his non-insolvency political risk claim before he can obtain the payment of loss compensation;

- price: a higher price is payable for higher market risks;
- protracted default: as stated previously, the period will also be impacted by the perceived market risks.

Generally, there are restrictions on terms of payment for C and D markets. Euler Hermes is generally not willing to grant open cover to debtors in countries with a D country rating. Cover on irrevocable letter of credit payment terms is possible, but this effectively means political risk cover only. Wider cover is, however, sometimes possible for large multinational companies operating in high-risk markets, when open credit will be assessed on a case-by-case basis and the experience of the exporter in trading in these markets.

TABLE 6.2 *Country ratings as applied by Euler Hermes (source: Euler Hermes, February 2012)*

EH rating	Number of countries	% of world GDP*	Definition
AA	39	66.0	Very low external transfer and convertibility risk; very strong business environment.
A	35	1.6	Low external transfer and convertibility risk; strong business environment.
BB	22	8.7	Moderate external transfer and convertibility risk; healthy, better-than-average business environment.
B	16	13.1	Significant external transfer and convertibility risk; less-than-average business environment.
C	50	3.0	High external transfer and convertibility risk; markedly less-than-average business environment.
D	79	4.5	Very high external transfer and convertibility risk; weak business environment.

(*) Only the countries in which the credit insurer has an interest (exposure) are monitored and awarded a rating. This implies that some countries are not followed up. For this reason only 96.9 % of the world GDP is affected by a country rating.

PART 3

The private credit insurance market

In chapter 7 we will offer a summary of the current situation in the private credit insurance market. In chapter 8 an attempt will be made to predict the future development of that market.

CHAPTER 7
THE PLAYERS AND THEIR PRODUCTS

The last ten to fifteen years have seen the private credit insurance market undergo a fundamental transformation through the amalgamation of various local companies at national level into one of three worldwide groups.

Market penetration is focussed on Western Europe, where 80% of the world's total credit insurance premiums are paid, on a penetration rate of approximately 15% of GDP. This is on the basis of the nominal value of covered commercial transactions.

1 The market situation in the private credit insurance sector

1.1 GENERAL

The creation of the single European market in 1993 acted as a catalyst for consolidation within the sector. This was further strengthened by the trend towards globalisation in the 1990s.

GOOD TO KNOW

As a consequence of increasing globalisation, the old – and relatively small – national credit insurance companies were no longer in a position to meet the new challenges on a stand-alone basis.

European companies began to export more and more to countries in Latin and South America, Africa and Asia. Reliable information was essential for the correct analysis of the credit risk, but the costs of obtaining this information grew dramatically as the distance increased. Greater synergy was the obvious solution.

In 2011, the turnover of the credit insurance sector amounted (according to ICISA figures) to roughly 7.2 billion euros.

1.2 THE BIG THREE

→ *Oligopoly*

The worldwide market is now dominated by a trio of large multinational companies, the so-called Big Three. In 2011 these companies – Euler Hermes, Coface and Atradius – controlled 79.2 % of the market (see figure 7.1).

Germany, France, the Netherlands, Belgium, UK, Italy and Spain all figure prominently in the present make-up of these three groups. Germany's Allianz Group has the major shareholding in Euler Hermes; Grupo Catalana Occidente is the leading shareholder in Atradius; and Natixis is the main shareholder in Coface.

FIGURE 7.1: *World market for private credit insurance in 2011, showing the International Credit Insurance and Surety Association's (ICISA) members; total market volume = circa 7.2 billion euros in premium receipts (source: Euler Hermes estimates)*

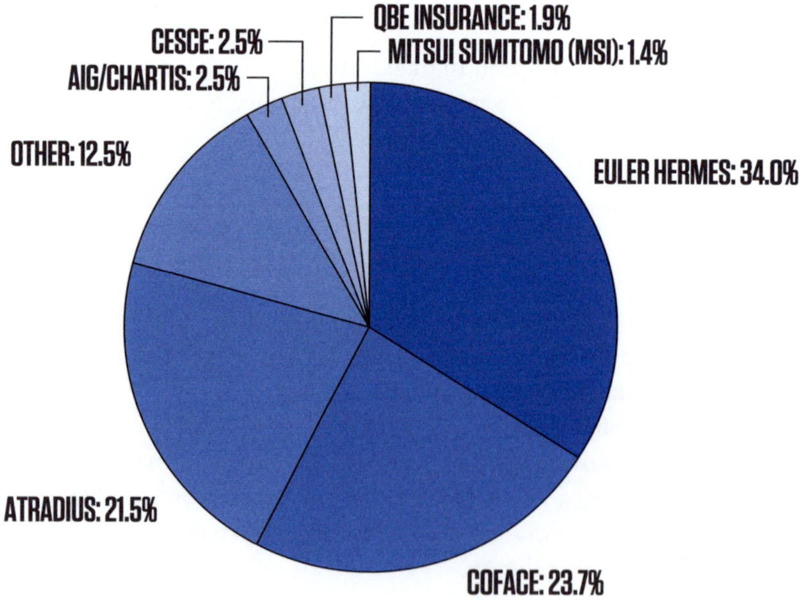

After the merger between Atradius and the Spanish Credito y Caucion in 2004, the first major wave of consolidation came to an end. This does not mean, however, that further, more minor consolidations will not continue to take place. The existence of these three large groups is a good example of the general consolidation effect that globalisation has had on the world economy.

The French have significant involvement in two of the three companies. Societe Francaise d'Assurance du Credit (SFAC) started out life as the principal French domestic credit insurer, before adopting its street-address name (Rue Euler). SFAC (the later Euler group) acquired e.g. the UK's Trade Indemnity Plc. Coface, on the other hand, was France's national Export Credit Agency, before being privatised in 1993. While the Euler Group subsequently purchased the Hamburg-based Hermes in 2002 (both belonging to the Allianz group), the privatised short-term arm of the UK's Export Credit Guarantee Department had first been purchased by Nederlandsche Credietverzekering Maatschapij (NCM) in 1991, and then merged with Gerling Konzern Speciale Kreditversicherung, to form Atradius in 2001. This Anglo-Dutch-German group was, in turn, purchased by the Spanish Credito y Caucion in 2004 (subsidiary of Grupo Catalane Occidente).

The German and Dutch companies had long been strong in their own buoyant economies and there had always been a well-established tradition of domestic credit insurance in France. The position of the UK as a major trading nation, exporting all over the world, meant that it was in the forefront of developing export credit and political risk cover in the private insurance market. Spain brought its influence in Portugal and South America to the convergence party.

The consolidation movement in the credit insurance sector, with its succession of fusions, take-overs and mergers, first needed to be submitted to the European Union for approval. The EU wanted to investigate whether or not the level of consolidation might not lead to unfair or distorted competition in certain countries and markets within the sector.

GOOD TO KNOW

In the numerous cases examined by the EU, the European Commission always came to the conclusion that the mergers were compatible with the requirements of the single market – and therefore gave their approval. The EU even went so far as to admit that 'many oligopolic markets display healthy levels of competition'.

→ *Euler Hermes*

This group was formed by successive acquisitions; SFAC (Societe Francaise d'Assurance du Credit) in France acquired Trade Indemnity Plc in the UK, and then the private arm of Hermes Kreditversicherung AG in Germany. The new holding company – Euler Hermes S.A., based in Paris – was set up in 2003.

Euler Hermes (*www.eulerhermes.com*) is the only credit insurer quoted on NYSE Euronext. (At the end of 1999 Coface was launched on the stock market in Paris, but its shares were later withdrawn in 2004).

Euler Hermes has concentrated on the development of its own internal information network. The Euler Hermes group pursues this policy by collecting important confidential information through various channels, which allows them to make more accurate credit decisions.

With a presence in over 50 countries, the Euler Hermes group has also developed a specific business model based on the premise that each local business unit (BU) or operational entity (OE) is responsible for collecting information relating to debtors in the countries where it operates. This has led to the creation of a large worldwide network. The BU also takes credit decisions in respect of these same debtors and carries out risk monitoring on behalf of all the insured parties throughout the group. This applies equally to the recovery of unpaid trade receivables in their countries. The business unit of the insured party, for whose debtors the credit limits are set by another local Euler Hermes branch, has the necessary means to protect the interests of the insured party, if required.

WHAT YOU NEED TO KNOW

This business model of Euler Hermes has not only led (understandably) to considerable synergy benefits but also (more importantly) to better information and better credit decisions. The risks are monitored by the local business units in accordance with the 'proximity of risk' principle. Because each BU acts on behalf of all the group's insured parties, greater pressure can be brought to bear on defaulting local debtors to pay what they owe. If payment is still not forthcoming, credit limits can also be reduced at local level. The consolidation of the credit insurance sector has therefore increased the impact that the insurers have on supplier credit.

→ *Coface*

Coface operates in 66 countries.

This company has taken shareholdings in a number of smaller credit insurance companies around the world, allowing it to grow to its present size.

Coface (*www.coface.fr*) is the only group that has also acquired local information agencies in all the main locations where it operates. In this way, Coface sought to achieve a certain degree of vertical integration, but this came to an end when the information activity was split out with the intention to sell.

Nevertheless, it remains a common theme across all three organisations that the collection of information and the recovery of unpaid trade receivables are carried out by local branches.

→ *Atradius*

Atradius has a presence in 45 countries.

The group was formed initially when the short-term business arm of the Dutch Nederlandsche Credietverzekering Maatschapij (NCM) purchased the privatised arm of the UK's Export Credit Guarantee Department in 1991. This company was in turn purchased by Gerling Kredit Speciale Kreditversicherung, based in Cologne, Germany. Following the deterioration of the financial position of Gerling's parent in Germany, as a result of its liabilities arising out of the telecom bubble in 2000 and the 9/11 disaster in New York, shareholders stepped in to merge the credit subsidiary with Credito y Caucion of Spain in 2004 (controlled by Grupo Cataluna).

Atradius (*www.atradius.com*) has a similar organisational structure to Euler Hermes: the collection of information, the underwriting of risks and credit monitoring are carried out for the group as a whole by a number of local offices (once again, on the 'proximity of risk' principle).

1.3 OTHER MARKET PLAYERS

In addition to the Big Three, there are a number of other important local players, such as Sace in Italy, Ethniki in Greece, CESCE in Spain, Ducroire in Belgium, R+V in Germany and FCIA (Foreign Credit Insurance Association) in the USA, etc. In 2012, Euler Hermes started a 50/50 joint venture with Mapfre, called Solunion. It will sell credit insurance policies in Spain and Latin America.

GOOD TO KNOW

Since the coming into force of the European Directive of 18 June 1992 relating to the freedom of movement of services, there have been a number of important shifts of emphasis in the credit insurance sector. Different international private credit insurers from outside Europe now find it easier to offer their services to the various member states of the Union. Nevertheless, the oligopoly of the Big Three has not been broken: the entrance threshold for newcomers is just too high.

1.4 CREDIT INSURANCE BROKERS

As in any industry, good product distribution is essential. Unlike other forms of insurance, which are legally required, credit insurance is entirely optional. Consequently, credit insurance policies need to be sold – and this requires someone to sell them. In the credit insurance sector, the brokers play a key role in this respect.

In France and the United Kingdom, for example, a staggering 90% of policies are sold by brokers. By contrast, in Belgium a large proportion of credit insurance policies are still sold directly by insurers themselves.

GOOD TO KNOW

The brokers who sell credit insurance policies are generally specialised in the field. This is necessary, given the specific nature of credit insurance, which requires an active contribution from all the various parties throughout the duration of the policy. As a result, credit insurance is a knowledge-intensive product (the brokers estimate that training takes about 3 years), which demands continuous follow-up (for example, the negotiation and monitoring of credit limits), as part of the all-important prevention policy.

The general insurance broker, who also sells other types of insurance policies (fire, theft, vehicle, etc.), has historically been only marginally interested in (and familiar with) credit insurance. With these other types of policy, the broker is usually only required to take action when damage or loss occurs; for example, after a house fire or a traffic accident.

Insurance brokers earn commission paid by the insurer, based on the premium paid by insured suppliers and companies. Obviously, the broker has to be appointed by his client, the insured customer of the credit insurance company. Brokers are legally bound to disclose upon request to their clients the amounts of commission they earn. Although paid by the credit insurer, the brokers see it as their first duty to work on behalf of the interests of their insured client. In this context, they sell the product to their clients and, in so doing, will examine the different policy proposals of the different credit insurers, providing advice to their clients about the relative merits of the different types of policy, prices and conditions, before recommending the 'best' option.

GOOD TO KNOW

From the standpoint of the credit insurer, the broker, by employing his own development, sales and technical staff, saves the credit insurer from the necessity of investing significant sums himself. The premium rates charged by the credit insurer, as we have seen, are calculated on the quality of the risks being offered, and are therefore the same whether a broker is appointed or not. The broker's services can therefore be considered as 'free' to the client.

In recent years, the role of brokers in the financial services sector has come under increasing scrutiny from regulators. Insurance brokers, and the way in which the market operates, have generally been given a clean bill of health and no changes have been recommended. Nevertheless, the brokers who sell financial plans and pensions, or who otherwise offer financial advice, are being increasingly prevented from earning commissions and are therefore having to charge fees for their services.

Because of the cost-intensive nature of their business, insurance brokers naturally tend to concentrate on selling credit insurance products to the larger companies, who, because of their larger turnover, will pay larger amounts of premium, from which the brokers' commissions are derived. The interests of SMEs are not totally overlooked, but, historically, this segment has been predominantly catered to by the direct business development teams of the credit insurers themselves.

2 Two international associations representing credit insurers

Two worldwide associations exist, whose task is to share experience and to represent the interests of their credit insurance underwriting members at international forums. They are:

1 ICISA (International Credit Insurance and Surety Association) acts for the private credit insurance sector. The 'Big Three' are great supporters of ICISA, and value the links it provides and the knowledge it imparts through its discussion platforms.
2 The Berne Union acts essentially for the public credit insurance sector, although some private credit insurers are also invited to participate. Its concerns are principally with country risk, but its remit also extends to ensuring that UN and inter-governmental policies are carried out (e.g., reining in the irresponsible selling of competitive cheap credit by the richer nations; or ensuring environmental concerns are taken into account when agreeing to support infrastructure projects, such as dams, etc.).

Both associations liaise with each other on all matters of common interest.

3 Market penetration in the private credit insurance sector

A frequently asked question is the extent to which private credit insurance has penetrated deeply into economic life in general. Statistics show that credit insurance (including sureties) accounts for between 1.5 and 2 % of the total non-life insurance turnover in Western Europe. These figures confirm the niche position of credit insurance within the insurance sector.

Other than this, there is relatively little data available in the public domain. One of the exceptions is the study carried out by the CEPS (Centre for European Policy Studies; Brussels) in 2001. Some of the figures are open to question, but they nevertheless give a broad impression of the sector's level of penetration throughout the EU.

Table 7.1 shows that in the United Kingdom in 2001 some 314 billion euros worth of trade transactions (domestic and export) were covered by credit insurance. The GDP reflects the value of all the goods and services produced in a country during one year, but there are elements of GDP that are not covered by private credit insurance (e.g. the public sector, intercompany transactions, etc.). It is not known how CEPS made its calculations. Nevertheless, it should be noted that the UK penetration rate of 19.7 % of GDP is relatively high, compared with the European average of 14.4 %. This is even more the case with exports, with a cover rate of 50.9 %. This figure seems unrealistically high; so high, in fact, that there must be some doubt about its accuracy.

TABLE 7.1 *Volume of covered trade transactions in 2001 (in millions of euros) and their share in GDP and export (source: CEPS)*

	Domestic	Export	Total	% of GDP insured	% of export insured
Austria*	12,000	16,325	28,325	13.8%	25.3%
Belgium	20,000	18,000	38,000	14.8%	8.5%
Denmark	8,300	14,400	22,700	12.5%	25.5%
Spain	80,000	18,000	98,000	15.1%	13.8%
France	160,000	54,000	214,000	14.7%	16.4%
Germany	130,000	65,000	195,000	9.4%	10.4%
Greece	1,530	717	2,247	1.7%	5.8%
Netherlands	Not known	Not known	93,950	21.8%	Not known
Portugal	7,000	7,000	14,000	11.5%	24.6%
UK	**158,000**	**156,000**	**314,000**	**19.7%**	**50.9%**
Total	*576,830*	*349,442*	*1,020,222*	*14.4%*	*19.8%*

(*) Year 2000

In general, it is assumed that the penetration rate should be around 15 % of GDP. But as already indicated, in reality market penetration is actually higher, since credit insurance does not (or rather, cannot) cover the full range of business transactions that take place within an economy, such as transactions involving the public sector (which represent an important part of GDP) and transactions between a mother company and its subsidiaries.

Only a relatively small part of market penetration originates from SMEs. This is strange, since it is precisely the smaller companies that have most to gain from such insurance: 33% of SMEs admit to having problems with payment arrears, with serious negative consequences for their cash-flow. For this reason,

80% of the SMEs have delayed deliveries to bad debtors at one time or another.

It is noticeable that only European countries appear in the table. Perhaps, however, this is not so surprising: the survey was carried out by a European institution into what is primarily a European phenomenon: 80% of all credit insurance premiums worldwide are paid in Europe and the continent has a very strong credit insurance culture.

FOOD FOR THOUGHT

Although there are no reliable recent figures, it seems likely that the market penetration of credit insurance in Europe has remained relatively static as a proportion of GDP, notwithstanding the fact that levels of world trade have risen considerably during the past two decades, even outside the OECD (see above). It would be interesting to research the reasons for this seeming anomaly.

4 Types of policy

In addition to the straightforward commercial risks whole turnover policy, it is also possible to distinguish other different types of policy in the private credit insurance sector: SME policies, excess of loss policies, credit management policies, investment policies, long-term policies, export credit policies (including political risks), and multinational policies. The three main credit insurers all offer a micro SME product, available online and primarily intended for companies with an annual turnover of less than 2 million euros. Above this figure, they offer a whole turnover product. These offerings vary from provider to provider. Larger companies are offered a rated policy with turnover declarations and transactional limit charges. There is also a multinational option for large global groups, with the risk underwriting taken on by local underwriters. Single buyer cover is also available, but on a selective basis.

4.1 SME POLICIES

The SME policy is a 'normal' credit insurance policy, which has simply been adjusted to meet the requirements of smaller and medium-sized businesses. Credit insurers differ with regard to the level at which they set their turnover ceilings.

The policy has simple notification and credit/claim application forms for the policyholders. The premium and the limit costs can be calculated and invoiced on a fixed-rate basis.

One of the main purposes of the policy is to keep administrative formalities to a minimum, whilst at the same time keeping costs as low as possible.

Nevertheless, the level of credit insurance penetration among SMEs remains relatively low. Interestingly, it is estimated that only 13% of the potential credit insurance market for SMEs has ever been covered. This figure has remained constant over a number of years. Hence the present recognition amongst credit insurers that it is necessary to explore other distribution channels and use alternative routes to reach this market.

Price appears to be the main stumbling block (including the administrative charges), followed by the conditions attached to the cover. To breathe new life into this potentially important market, credit insurers are currently in the process of devising a series of new policy formulae to try and meet these objectives.

4.2 STANDARD WHOLE TURNOVER POLICIES

The targets for these policies are generally companies with a turnover of minimum 5 million euros, for which an SME policy is not suitable. The entire customer trade debtor portfolio is offered for insurance. Exemptions and exclusions are possible, following consultation and mutual agreement, but always on the basis of objective criteria (certain sectors, particular countries, etc.).

This is the most standard – and therefore the most popular – type of policy in credit insurance.

4.3 EXCESS OF LOSS POLICIES

The target companies for aggregate excess of loss cover are usually those with a turnover of minimum 10 million euros, who wish to reduce costs. This is also a whole turnover product as standard. With this type of policy, claims are only paid once an agreed annual aggregate excess of loss figure has been exceeded, following which all claims then qualify for payment. There is normally a non-qualifying loss (say 5,000 euros), under which claims are not considered.

Some credit insurers have gone further in developing this product, allowing them to better cater to the needs of larger companies. (Euler Hermes now has such an offering for companies with a turnover in excess of 100 million euros.)

4.4 CREDIT MANAGEMENT POLICIES

Not all credit insurers offer this product. It is a defensive product, targeted at companies with a turnover of at least 25 million euros per annum and which possess:

- a structured credit management system approved by the credit insurer (following an audit, where necessary);
- the required skilled staff and measuring instruments to ensure effective monitoring and analysis of customer risk;
- a financial structure capable of absorbing the average rate of loss over the past five years.

In accordance with a series of internal procedural rules, the insured party will then assess the solvency of his own customers independently, will have the right to set new credit limits, will monitor his own debtors and will collect outstanding debts. In these circumstances, trust and good communication between the insured party and the insurer are an essential prerequisite.

This type of policy is also linked to a larger annual aggregate excess of loss limit, which requires the insured party to accept the loss for claims up to that level. In fact, the objective of both the insurer and the insured party with a policy of this type is to provide cover against exceptional losses only, so that the policy is often alternatively known as a catastrophe policy.

In principle, only formally declared (official) insolvencies are covered. In exceptional cases, however, claims on the basis of protracted default can also be allowed. The level of cover with such policies is usually 90% (or in some cases even 100%) of the net loss in excess of the agreed annual aggregate limit.

The premium is based on a fixed rate and must be paid in advance. In principle, there are no limit/study costs, since the insured party does not ask the insurer to set any credit limits.

Some credit insurers specialise almost exclusively in the sale of this type of policy. They argue that the classic credit insurance policy is too expensive and administratively too time-consuming for larger companies. Nevertheless, prospective clients must also be aware that in order to enjoy the benefits of a credit management policy they must first fulfil three conditions to the satisfaction of the insurer:

- they must possess adequate and well-developed credit management systems;
- they must possess a good general company organisation;

→ they must have an excellent knowledge of their customers/debtors.

In contrast to the standard global (whole turnover) credit insurance policy, risk prevention is not the insurer's first concern with a credit management policy, since this task is delegated (to a large extent) to the insured party. Experience also shows that companies paying a substantial premium with no return – because annual losses fall under the excess of loss limit – can often become disillusioned with this concept. There is certainly a pattern of customers returning to more standard global cover.

Euler Hermes does not offer this product, as such. It does, however, offer a variant of the whole turnover policy, which sets a limit (say 50,000 euros) with named buyers only, all exposure in excess of this limit being covered. Because of the degree of selection involved, there is a significant price impact on cover of this type.

HOW IT WORKS

It is a fact that the large majority of major international companies – even companies that possess their own competent credit management departments – have a preference for the more classic type of credit insurance policy. They regard the close collaboration with the insurer that these policies entail as a clear added value. A credit management policy is not intended for use by SMEs.

4.5 INVESTMENT POLICIES

Investment policies are issued by national export credit agencies and political risk insurers (e.g. Lloyd's of London) to offer cover against confiscation or nationalisation of investments made overseas. These are not trade credit policies as such, but are designed to protect companies from having the loss of their assets inadequately compensated by the overseas government in question. They are (inevitably) long-term policies over many years.

4.6 LONG-TERM POLICIES

Major projects, capital goods and certain types of product (e.g. ships and aircraft), invariably involving multi-million currency deals, are unique and complex matters. This is equally true of the larger mixed goods/works contracts. Policies covering single major deals of this type are, once again, generally the preserve of the national export credit agencies. Such policies necessarily involve long periods of credit. Berne Union countries have agreed basic norms for the length of credit for certain products (e.g. ships and aircraft), which can sometimes exceed the desired maximum of 5 years.

In recent years, the private sector has shown increasing willingness to offer its own cover in this field.

4.7 EXPORT CREDIT POLICIES (INCLUDING POLITICAL RISKS)

These policies are normally whole turnover in nature and involve short terms of payment. The policies are specifically designed for exporting companies, and not only cover the insolvency and protracted default risks of non-payment by the buyer, but also a range of contract frustration risks (such as war, civil war, inconvertibility of exchange, new import restrictions, etc.), which may arise as a result of the actions of the buyer's or of a third party government or public authority. Premium is usually paid on a declaring basis, whilst the rates will vary according to the countries to which goods are being exported (see chapter 6, section 4).

4.8 MULTINATIONAL POLICIES

The growth of the global economy means that more and more multinational companies are opening business units in different continents.

DON'T DO IT!

In the past, local business units used to seek cover from local credit insurers. In a multinational context, this meant that a single large group might have several different polices, each with a different structure and conditions. This makes it more difficult to implement a uniform credit management policy throughout the organisation as a whole, which is crucial for the optimisation of consolidated working capital.

For this reason, credit insurers now offer a range of multinational programmes, providing group-wide or worldwide policy cover under the same conditions, irrespective of the location of the business units. Nevertheless, each local BU still has access to a local support service run by the insurer's own local branch office for the purposes of credit limit adjustment/approval and the collection of outstanding debts.

This type of policy has become much easier to organise and administer in recent years, thanks to the global consolidation of the credit insurance sector.

4.9 SPECIAL CASES

→ *Top-up cover*

Again, this type of cover may not be available from all credit insurers. Euler Hermes and Coface offer this product, alongside a traditional whole turnover product. The Euler Hermes CAP Europe policy enables an existing policyholder to pay extra premium for a specific limit, separate from their existing cover, subject to certain (often individual) criteria being met. In exceptional circumstances (for example, when one insurer is at the limit of his capacity), it may be possible for another insurer to top up the cover given under the original policy (although this will probably be an expensive option).

GOOD TO KNOW

In general, credit insurers are not in favour of multi-provider top-up arrangements. This is related to the fundamental credit insurance principle that only a maximum percentage of the risk should be covered, in order to ensure that the insured party continues to monitor the risks diligently and assertively. This same principle applies equally to the reduction of existing credit limits or the partial acceptance of new credit applications. Top-up cover can also lead to other (often complex) problems with regard to recoveries after a loss compensation claim has been submitted, when there needs to be a proportional division of any money recovered between the (now usually more than one) insurer and the insured party.

→ *Cover for single trade credit risks*

One of the basic principles of credit insurance is that the totality of the customer's turnover should be offered for insurance, so that the insurer accepts a mixture of good and bad risks – and not just the bad ones!

This having been said, occasionally cover is requested for an isolated single risk. The resulting policies are referred to variously as single risk policies, single transaction policies or single buyer policies. They are applicable in the following circumstances:

- → an exceptional or disproportionate transaction in relation to the value of the customers overall book of business;
- → exposure to a particular market risk (usually political);
- → a delivery of capital goods;
- → when cover of this kind is demanded by the bank financing the transaction.

Nevertheless, single risk cover remains the exception rather than the rule in the private credit insurance sector. As mentioned previously, public credit insurers accept single risks more frequently to cover long-term credit in countries outside the OECD zone.

CHAPTER 8
CHALLENGES FOR THE FUTURE

As already mentioned in chapter 7, the private credit insurance market in Europe has already gained a large share of the non-SME corporate market. There is also fierce price competition between the major credit insurers. The need to tie in with banks and other introducers has meant the growth of many different programmes in the market place in recent times, in an attempt to convert more companies to credit insurance in preference to self-insurance and the creation of bad debt reserves.

The credit insurance policy has a special character. The current product is the result of the experiences of the past 150 years. Until recently, developments of the product and the services it offered were significantly greater in the political risk arena than in the commercial risk arena. Now, however, things are beginning to change here also.

Other offerings – such as the selling of information, no limits policies, collections, faster claims payments, tracking and monitoring of the sales ledger, pro-actively letting clients know when cover is available on buyers, etc. – have all added to the benefits of credit insurance in recent times. Attempts are increasingly being made to broaden the appeal of the credit insurance policy, allowing it to reach audiences not previously targeted.

The sector is now looking at other possible ways to expand its field of operations. There is a recognition that more attention needs to be devoted to the development of better policies for SMEs. In addition to their insurance activities, there is also scope for credit insurers to develop other related initiatives, for which they will receive payment on a commission basis. For example, they might provide a packaged service for company credit management activities. Technological developments are also opening new doors of opportunity.

1 The current environment

The effects of the global financial crisis of 2008-2009 continue to rumble on. Declining turnover in many sectors, and particularly a contraction in the construction sector, has seen levels of insured turnover decline.

Moreover, as a consequence of increased competition on the one hand and the consolidation of the sector during recent decades (with its resulting increase in efficiency) on the other hand, the levels of premium in recent years have fallen significantly. They now vary between 0.1 and 1%, dependent on the specific risk profile of the debtor portfolio of the insured party.

1.1 FIERCE COMPETITION

It is possible to speak of a fiercely competitive climate. This expresses itself in two distinct ways:

1. Notwithstanding the fact that the credit insurance market has been described as an oligopoly, there is a constant and hard-fought price war between the different companies and groups.
2. As mentioned above, there has been a growing tendency towards self-insurance (autonomously managed in-house). By purchasing trade information reports and adjusting their IT-systems, some companies now consider that they have the necessary expertise to replace the credit insurers, through the building up of financial reserves that will allow them to absorb any losses from bad debts that may occur. Companies that embark on this course (probably in the belief it will save costs), but without having the requisite resources or expertise in place, are exposing themselves to the greater danger of operating unprotected in the wild waters of the present global economy.

GOOD QUESTION

Should credit insurers regard factoring companies as being part of the competition? The answer to this question is both 'yes' and 'no'. On the one hand, 'yes': in addition to covering credit risks, like a credit insurer, factors also offer default management and the financing of trade receivables as part of their service. On the other hand, 'no': the covering of credit risks usually takes place in collaboration with a credit insurer, so that credit insurance and factoring can better be regarded as complementary in this respect. The cooperation between credit insurance and factoring takes mostly place within the context of non-recourse factoring (i.e. factoring with insurance built in).

1.2 SELF-INSURANCE

Self-insurance is the internal financing of future risks, as opposed to their external financing through the payment of premiums to a third party: the credit insurer.

Companies considering the autonomous self-insurance of their trade receivables must, however, bear the following points in mind:

- the funds that are used to build up the necessary reserves (from their own capital) are not deductible from the result of the profit-and-loss account;
- the reserves can only be allocated after tax on the result;
- it is not always easy to build up reserves of the necessary scale; this is dependent on whether the company books a profit in the year in question;
- the reserves booked into the company account are not separate; in other words, they are not explicitly allocated to the coverage of a specific risk that might occur in the future; provisions on the liabilities side of the account can only be set aside when it is possible to identify their allocation to a specific risk in the financial year in question;
- the funds that are used to create the reserve are often invested in paper securities, which cannot always be converted into cash with a profit; this is dependent on the state of the market;
- a (family) company does not always have the required discipline to build up the level of reserves that is necessary to cover future default risks; the temptation to pay out a dividend is often too great;
- it is not possible to take out reinsurance, unless the company has set up a 'captive' (see below).

2 New challenges for the credit insurance product

The financial and economic crisis of 2008-2009 sent shockwaves throughout the entire sector. As the credit insurers were confronted with a sharp rise in their loss ratios, the value of the product became the subject of much discussion and many debtors criticised a serious lack of communication, when credit limits were either reduced or withdrawn. In the middle of the worst financial crisis in 50 years, the insurers were not well informed about the real liquidity position of the debtors – and insolvency can be brought about all too quickly by insufficient liquidity. This must also be viewed with regard to changes in insolvency legislation in the past decade which have made it easier for firms to enter a form of insolvency in the UK. The so-called 'pre-pack' administration process has not been friendly to the credit insurers.

The economic situation being faced today is not all that different. However, credit insurers are now conducting steady rather than drastic reviews of the limits on their books. Dealing with the economic shocks of recent years has left credit insurers much better informed to make the decisions that can best protect both their policyholders and their shareholders alike. In the Euler Hermes case, this is reflected in the S & P rating of AA- and in its position as being part of the world's leading insurer: Allianz.

2.1 CODE OF CONDUCT

Regulators in most countries require credit insurers (like all other insurance companies) to comply with an agreed code of conduct.

The code imposes obligations on both parties:
- The insured party undertakes, for example, to do his best to collect as much information as possible about the debtor and to provide this information to the credit insurer. This is in keeping with the pre-existing notification obligation, and allows the credit insurer to assess the credit risks reliably and in full.
- The credit insurer undertakes to justify the reduction or withdrawal of credit limits as fully as possible.

Communication must be efficient and effective.

2.2 MODERNISATION OF THE PRODUCT

→ *From difficult beginnings*

Credit insurance has existed since the 19th century. In Jean Bastin's book on credit insurance, there is a chapter about the history of the sector, which discusses the origins of today's current product. Bastin shows that, at first, things were very difficult for the credit insurers. It was only by gradual trial and error that it was finally possible to develop a workable product that combined the solvency and profitability that was necessary to guarantee the market's future.

HOW IT WORKS

In essence, the commercial risk credit insurance product has changed very little during the last half century. During this same period the world has undergone a metamorphosis. Nevertheless, it must not be overlooked that in operational matters the sector has also made huge advances during the past 50 years. In particular, the consolidation process of recent decades has resulted in considerable benefits for both insurer and insured. This applies equally to the introduction of credit ratings for debtors.

GOOD TO KNOW

Insurers are constantly searching for a 'blue ocean' product. However, in the UK, with its high proliferation of specialist brokers, any successful innovation is soon copied by the competition. An insurer with huge global resources should, nonetheless, still be able to maintain a competitive advantage. Euler Hermes's offering of risk offices with unique access to first-hand buyer data is a very good example of this.

→ *Some suggestions for improvement*

The crisis of 2008-2009 demonstrated all too clearly that the current structure of the product has a number of weaknesses, which need to be improved. In Belgium a Think Tank (facilitated by the broker AON/Crion) was created, which in December 2012 published a white paper on credit insurance, with proposals from the market for improvement and innovation.

a ***The problem of nominal credit limits: too much 'fat' or 'air'?***

In terms of a fixed premium product, exposure on credit limits often far exceeds the real total turnover of the insured party. This leads to a review of the limits in place at the next renewal. Companies tendering for business will frequently hold on to unnecessary cover, even when they fail to be awarded the business. It is estimated that as little as one third of total exposure relates to real exposure for insurers (but this figure is very approximate).

USEFUL TIPS

One possible innovation in this respect is to require the insured party to pay a premium on the full amount of the credit limit. If he no longer needs this full amount, this would prompt him to cancel the balance that is now surplus to his requirements. This principle has already been applied in some European countries. Another option might be to introduce a commitment fee for unused limits (as is currently the case with bank credits).

GOOD TO KNOW

These measures would have helped to cut the number of reductions made by the insurers during the 2008-2009 crisis (which led to a negative perception in the market). During this difficult period, some insurers imposed reductions of between 30% and 50%, but the real effect and relevance of these reductions was minimal, since large parts of the original nominal limits were simply not being used: they contained too much 'fat'. Unfortunately, the insurers allowed themselves to be sucked into this negative spiral, even though they had not actually been able to reduce the real level of risk. For debtors, however, the reductions certainly made things difficult, and the market began to question exactly why the credit insurers suddenly considered them to be significantly less creditworthy. In short, an almost 'panic' reduction of credit limits simply served to create more volatility, thereby depressing the general market climate still further.

Another aspect of this same situation is Solvency II, to which the credit insurance market is subject. In this context, it is important to know the extent of the real covered risk (in other words, the use of the nominal limits) in order to calculate the risk allocated capital (RAC).

The solution for this problem must be a pragmatic one, taking due account of the fact that there are seasonal effects in many sectors, which may make higher temporary limits necessary at different times of the year.

b *The issuing of notice for credit reductions and withdrawals*
Until recently, the credit insurer was able to reduce or revoke credit limits with immediate effect. This sometimes placed both the policyholder and his buyers in a difficult position. Increasingly, however, credit insurers (e.g., Euler Hermes) have introduced a delayed effect clause, which allows policyholders a 30 day period of grace in this scenario.

In some other cases, credit insurers now give notice of their intent to reduce or revoke.

c *Certificate of credit management*
Credit management is still undervalued in most companies. A positive way to change this situation might be to introduce a certificate of good credit management, assessed and issued by an independent third party. This could be included, for example, in the annual audit.

GOOD ADVICE

The company in question would have to pay for this certificate. But in exchange for this clear indication of good management, it may be possible for credit insurers to grant holders of the certificate a lower level of premium and greater autonomy to set their own credit limits.

Such companies would be less dependent on regular dialogue with the insurer, which should significantly reduce administration costs. Under the terms of Basle II/III, the banks could consider similarly rewarding companies, by giving them a better internal rating and a lower interest margin on their borrowing requirements.

3 Broadening horizons

By broadening horizons we mean first and foremost making the product more popular with and suitable for SMEs. A secondary focus must be the further development of so-called fee business.

3.1 SMEs (SMALL AND MEDIUM-SIZED BUSINESS)

The European Union has devoted considerable attention to the definition of an SME. In order to belong to one of the three SME categories, it is necessary (according to the EU) to satisfy two of the three threshold conditions (see table 8.1).

TABLE 8.1 *Different categories of SME (source: European Union)*

	Micro-entity	Small company	Medium-sized company
Turnover (in euros)	2,000,000	8,800,000	35,000,000
Balance total (i.e., net assets in euro)	2,000,000	4,400,000	17,500,000
Number of employees	10	50	250

The definition is a broad one: few people would regard a turnover of 35 million euros as being medium-sized. When we talk about SMEs, most people tend to think of the small companies and micro-entities with a turnover of less than 8.8 million euros.

Of all companies, the SMEs are probably the ones that could benefit most from credit insurance as a useful support for their own credit management procedures. In reality, however, very few SMEs currently make use of this valuable instrument. Only 2% of small companies currently have a credit insurance policy, in contrast to 30% of large companies (according to a 2006 Sigma study from Swiss Re about credit insurance and surety). In other words, there is still a huge potential market to be exploited: in Europe alone, there are more than 25 million SMEs. In fact, in many countries they are seen as the lifeblood of the national economy.

Credit insurers are attempting to improve this situation by bringing onto the market a new range of simple policies. Some are trialling products on the basis of web-applications via the internet, for which both the premiums and the study costs are charged at a fixed rate. This significantly reduces overall administration costs.

Euler Hermes has just introduced a new product – 'Simplicity' – to the UK market for companies with a turnover up to £4 million, offering 60% indemnity as standard and no named credit limits. The idea is to attract these companies to the more standard offering. In other words, 'Simplicity' is a taster policy.

GOOD TO KNOW

It is a major challenge to find the right distribution channels. The credit insurer must be able to make use of a network of partners to bring his product to the different sectors of the market. This network might include the large financial institutions (with their numerous branch offices), professional associations, brokers, etc.

3.2 FEE BUSINESS

Credit insurers see limit charges as falling into this category. For many years, credit insurers wrapped up all their charges in a single premium rate. However, this premium attracted insurance premium tax and reinsurance costs. By separately charging for information and monitoring, they have been able to manage the costs of risk premium much better and have provided themselves with a better base for the necessary investment in IT and technology development.

A fee or commission for the provision of a service is another remuneration that does not increase the level of risk in the credit insurer's portfolio. Through synergies and economies of scale, he might well be able to offer these services relatively cheaply (for example, services that cover the full cycle of a trade account, such as rating information, credit management advice, debt recovery, etc).

→ *Should we fear cannibalisation?*

There is an argument that the above-mentioned diversification might lead to the cannibalisation of the core product: the credit insurance policy. If premium income should become sufficiently reduced, in such a way as to allow other forms of fee income to grow, this could have serious ramifications elsewhere (e.g. in the reinsurance market).

Yet no matter what information the credit insurer has at his disposal, at the moment of making a limit decision the risk of non-payment will always be present.

WHAT YOU NEED TO KNOW

The insurance aspect of credit insurance will always retain its value, come what may. When a credit limit is mistakenly given to a defaulting debtor during a preventative risk analysis, the insurer will accept his responsibility and pay claims compensation. After all, no one can be right all the time. The number of household names (such as Woolworths, Comet, HMV, etc.) that have failed in recent times should make credit insurance even more of an attractive proposition. Nowadays, even blue chip companies are at risk of failure.

But is it not possible that in this rapidly changing world other market players might try to break into the core business of the credit insurance sector? If credit insurers remain too passive they run the risk that other bolder spirits might pull the rug out from under their feet. At the present time, the entrance threshold for outsiders is too high, but it might not always be this way – particularly if further technological advances cut costs even further.

→ *Some possibilities*

a ***Information: the ratings***

From a moral point of view, it is not always easy (or possible) for a credit insurer to sell complete versions of his information reports to third parties. This information has been collected from a variety of different and often confidential sources, who might consider breaking off the network relationship, if they thought that their 'contributions' might be made public.

Having said this, the credit insurer does possess a unique store of information, which can be of considerable added value to others. (Euler Hermes, for example, has 56,000 insured parties, whose combined payment experiences of debtors around the globe are potentially of great value to numerous other operators in the financial and credit markets.)

It is clear that the credit insurance sector must focus on information that originates from its core activity and that the customer cannot find elsewhere, but without in any way detracting from the confidential nature of certain details; in particular, the ratings. Anyway, procured information from commercial information agencies can't be sold by the insurers to third parties for contractual reasons.

b ***Recovery/collection***

In view of their experience and know-how, it is logical that the credit insurers will gradually move further and further into this field of activity. Euler Hermes Collections is already the UK's largest debt collector, available to insured and non-insured parties.

GOOD TO KNOW

In this context, we must make a distinction between claims (recovery for insured parties) and collections (recovery for other third parties). In this latter respect, it is clear that the credit insurers will be entering into increasing competition with legal offices, debt collection agencies, etc.

It is also possible to take matters a step further by buying up unredeemed debts from the creditors for a proportion of their nominal value (discount). Some years ago, the Belgian state already sold off some of its most difficult to recover tax debts to third parties.

c ***Credit management***

Credit management is the next logical progression. The credit insurer's skills in credit monitoring and debt recovery, coupled with his knowledge of the legal regulations in numerous countries, make him the ideal person to provide advice and assistance to companies in their own credit management operations.

Why should the insurer confine himself to the provision of loss cover through the sale and administration of an insurance policy? He is perfectly capable of setting 'advisory' credit limits for third parties, who do not necessarily need to be insured parties. The only difference is that in this case he has no responsibility to accept the loss. Alternatively, he could agree to a limited degree of cover, say 20%, to demonstrate a level of commitment commensurate with that of a credit insurer.

PART 4

Return and importance

This is a hugely important part of the book. In the next two chapters we will look at the following points of interest.

- *In chapter 9 we will examine the financial importance of credit insurance. The starting point for this examination is the insured supplier. This chapter also has a micro-economic orientation. What is the real return on a credit insurance policy?*
- *In chapter 10 we will examine the economic importance of credit insurance. Through its impact on the working capital and liquidity of a company, credit insurance has great macro-economic influence. We will illustrate this point with a case study – although the truth of the matter has already been proven time and again during the financial and economic crisis of 2008-2009.*

GOOD TO KNOW

With this approach, we will be placing the emphasis on the management of a company's working capital. We will deal with this subject at length, since it is closely related to both the core importance of private credit insurance and the need for good credit management. Investment in working capital has received increasing attention in the world of financial management in recent years, a process that was accelerated during the financial and economic crisis of 2008-2009, and continues to the present day.

Working capital is the capital of a company that is used for the continuous, day-to-day running of the business activity through the financing of stocks and trade receivables, in contrast to the capital that is used for long-term investments.

CHAPTER 9
THE FINANCIAL IMPORTANCE OF CREDIT INSURANCE

In this chapter we will discuss a number of points of interest that will give a clearer understanding of the return on the premium for a credit insurance policy. First and foremost, trade credit has opportunity costs. Credit insurance can contribute towards the more efficient management of working capital and also to a healthier balance sheet structure and better returns. In this context, credit insurance must be seen as an important instrument of support for the effective credit management of the insured party.

1 Trade receivables are an important but sensitive balance sheet item

Trade receivables are shown on the assets side of the balance sheet, as part of the current assets. For the company, they represent an important investment in its working capital: on average, they form 16.5% of the balance total in UK, but in some countries of Southern Europe this can easily increase to 30% of the total assets (see figure 9.1). In France, the total volume of trade credit amounts to some 300 billion euros or twice the volume of short-term bank credits. In fact, we might even say that the supplier is acting de facto as a banker and that companies in general are larger external financiers than the banks. The weight of the trade receivables on the balance sheet is linked to the payment tenor: the longer the tenor, the more important the weight (see chapter 2). This means that the impact of trade receivables on the balance sheet is greater in Southern Europe than in Northern Europe, because the payment tenor in Southern Europe is much longer than in the North. The United Kingdom is somewhere in the middle.

The risk of suffering a major loss increases in proportion to the level of turnover, while the financial capability to bear this loss decreases in the same proportion. Above all, start-up companies in rapid growth are particularly vulnerable and need to remain alert.

FIGURE 9.1 *Typical balance sheet of a company (source Euler Hermes)*

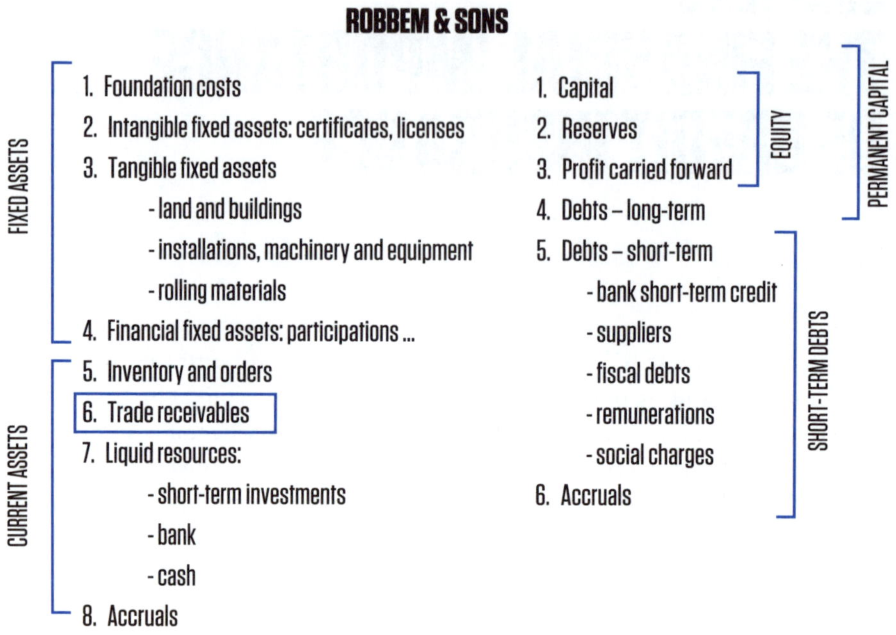

One should also bear in mind that Pareto's Law – otherwise known as the 80/20 rule – usually applies: 20% of customers are responsible for 80% of a company's turnover. This means that a serious loss in respect of one of these key 20% of customers can have a huge negative impact on working capital.

FOOD FOR THOUGHT

No one questions the need for fire insurance to cover our homes and possessions. We keep on doing this, even though the chance of a fire is small, because we know that if there ever is a fire it will then be too late to do anything about insurance! It is therefore puzzling that so many people seem to doubt the need to take out credit insurance to protect their trade receivables from the risk of default.

Moreover, we should not forget that in addition to the so-called predictable risks – risks that we can detect by conducting a thorough investigation of a debtor's financial credentials – there are also other unforeseen risks that a businessman can do little about, and against which he is largely defenceless. We only have to look at the collapse of the US sub-prime mortgage market and its knock-on effects across the world in 2008-2009 to acknowledge this. As a result of the subsequent collapse of bank lending and market confidence generally, companies were caught out by a reduction in the size of their sales markets and the increase in the level of their inventory/stock, all of which led to cash-flow problems. In these circumstances, debtors inevitably asked their suppliers for the deferment of payment. When this type of negative development occurs, the circulation and growth of new trade credit, on which economic prosperity depends, almost grinds to a halt.

2 The cost price of customer credit

We will look at the cost price of customer credit from two different perspectives:

- → Cash payment or payment on delivery: how much does it cost to offer a discount of x% if the customer is prepared to pay in cash (on delivery)? Is this a viable alternative for the deferment of payment? In addition to the financial aspects of the situation, this discount can also be seen as a form of self-protection against the credit risk presented by the debtor.
- → Payment period: how much do we save by shortening the payment period and how much do we lose by making it longer? This is concerned with the financial aspects of trade credit.

2.1 CASH PAYMENT (ON DELIVERY)

A supplier wants to be paid as quickly as possible: in this way he will have the necessary liquidity to maintain or improve his treasury and cash-flow position. The possibility of loss through the insolvency of the debtor disappears immediately if the debt is settled in cash (on delivery).

To persuade the buyer to agree to cash payment, the supplier sometimes offers an interesting discount on the sale price. But this discount represents an important cost item in the profit & loss (P&L) account, a fact that is often overlooked.

Let us assume a normal payment period of 60 days, with a possible discount of 2% if the account is settled in full within 10 days (this is the same as cash or on delivery payment, being 50 days quicker than the normal payment period). There are two different ways that the cost price can be calculated: the simple method and the method with compound interest.

→ *The simple method*

2% for 50 days (60 days – 10 days) can be transformed into a P&L cost as follows. Starting with an invoice of 100, a discount of 2 is applied, which is then related to the difference between both these figures, namely 98 (100 – 2):

$$\frac{2}{98} \times \frac{360}{50} = 14.69\%$$

The first factor (2/98) implies that the cost over a period of 50 days will be equivalent to 2.04% of the invoice total (in this case, 98). The second factor (360/50) spreads this cost over a year: how many times each year can this cost of 2.04% be incurred. Based on a shortening of the payment period by 50 days, this means that these costs can be incurred 7.2 (or 360/50) times per annum.

The formula is therefore:

$$\text{Nominal annual cost} = \frac{\text{discount \%}}{100 - \text{discount \%}} \times \frac{360}{\text{number of days credit} - \text{'cash' period}}$$

→ *The method with compound interest*

The simple method takes no account of compound interest; i.e., the time value of the money for the period that it has been paid out earlier (after 2 months instead of a year). An interest rate of 2% over 2 months is not equivalent to 12% per annum, but based on the compound interest rate it becomes: $(1.02)^6 = 12.62\%$.

The correct method of calculation for the annual cost of a discount of 2% is therefore $(1+2/98)^{360/50} - 1 = 15.66\%$. Consequently, this is higher than the 14.69% of the previous method.

The formula here is:

$$\text{Actual annual cost} = \left(1 + \frac{\text{discount \%}}{100 - \text{discount \%}}\right)^{\frac{360}{\text{credit period} - \text{'cash' period}}} - 1$$

Table 9.1 (based on the compound interest method) shows that the global discount costs are higher for both shorter payment periods and higher discount rates.

TABLE 9.1 *Annual costs – compound interest (source: FECMA – Federation of European Credit Management Associations)*

Days	2% discount	3% discount	4% discount
30	27.43	44.12	63.21
40	19.94	31.54	44.40
50	15.66	24.52	34.17
60	12.89	20.05	27.75

→ *The supplier's choice*

The supplier therefore needs to ask himself whether or not the discount costs for cash payment are worth it in comparison with the possible revenue he can earn from his available capital, and also in terms of the price he is willing to pay for the covering of the credit risk.

1 ***Revenue from available capital.***
This can be verified on the basis of current market rates of interest. If the current market rate is around 4% and the annual costs for a 2% discount amount to 15.66%, the discount in question is a very expensive one for the supplier. In other words, the amount that the supplier has deducted from his invoice (the discount) is not compensated by the financial return (rate of interest on capital) as a result of the earlier settlement of trade receivables. Of course, this is looking at things purely from the supplier's point of view.

BE SMART

The customer/buyer stands on the other side of this equation: for him, cash payment can often be very beneficial. It is for this reason that some companies prefer to make use of other forms of short-term credits rather than trade credit, so that they can pay cash (on delivery) – and profit from the discount.

Some buyers/debtors do not have this option available to them, because their creditworthiness is not good enough to secure other short-term financing alternatives. This means that they are 'forced' to rely on supplier credit (at least as long as their creditworthiness is reasonable), and therefore *de facto* pay opportunity costs by not being able to capitalise on the discount offer.

2 ***The price the supplier is willing to pay to eliminate the credit risk, or the risk of non-payment on the due date of payment***
This aspect requires us to take account of the estimated cost of credit insurance. From a fiscal perspective, discounts for cash payments are seen as a financial cost and are therefore deductible. This applies equally, however, to credit insurance premiums. Nevertheless, the above example shows that a discount cost of 15.66% (or net 11.66% per annum, following deduction of 4% earned interest) is a very expensive alternative to the payment of a credit insurance premium, which can range from sub 0.1% to (sometimes, but seldom above) 1% on the realised insured turnover.

2.2 SHORTENING OF THE PAYMENT PERIOD

It is sometimes easily overlooked, but a shortening of the payment period can yield the supplier a significant financial gain. Because his money is made available to him more quickly, his treasury and cash-flow position improves considerably.

This benefit can be calculated for a full year with the following formula:

$$\left| \frac{\text{Turnover}}{(360/OP)} - \frac{\text{Turnover}}{(360/NP)} \right| \times \frac{r}{100}$$

where:
Turnover = annual turnover
OP = original payment period
NP = new payment period
r = market rate of interest

The annual turnover divided by the fraction (360/OP) gives the average initial investment in the working capital (via trade receivables) throughout that year. If the maximum payment period is shortened, the investment in working capital falls. This leads to a cash-flow benefit.

Applied to an annual turnover of 1 million euros and a payment period reduced from 60 days (OP) to 40 days (NP), the additional gain in terms of working capital will be as follows:

1,000,000/ (360/60) = 1,000,000/6 = 166,667 euros
1,000,000/ (360/40) = 1,000,000/9 = 111,111 euros

In other words, on an annual basis we would invest an average of 55,556 euros (166,667 – 111,111) less in our working capital, if we cut the length of the payment period by 20 days. If we invest this amount for the full year at an interest rate of 4%, this results in additional financial income of 2,222 euros, which is good for the return of the company.

GOOD TO KNOW

It is self-evident that the results obtained by shortening the maximum payment period will vary according to the total amount of turnover on the one hand and the proportional reduction of the payment period on the other hand. The rate of interest is another important variable factor.

We shall see later that the relationship between the supplier and his customer is not threatened by the application of this measure. On the contrary, the supplier's professional approach earns him greater respect than before.

2.3 COMMERCIAL CONSIDERATIONS

Of course, things are not always as simple as in the example above. The payment period is only one aspect of the commercial negotiations that take place between the supplier and his customer. And each country and each sector has its own specific customs and usages.

This is something that should not be overlooked when concluding a credit insurance policy, within the framework of wider support for a credit management system.

FOOD FOR THOUGHT

It is useful to be aware of the above. Customer credit always contains a (hidden) financial cost and in this sense is never 'free'. And this is before we even consider the possible default risk of the debtor: the longer the payment period, the greater the risk of non-payment.

3 Cover against exceptional loss on trade receivables

Credit insurance covers the non-payment risk that the supplier runs with regard to his customers/debtors. This represents both the commercial and the financial importance of the policy for the insured party.

Table 9.2 clearly illustrates the impact that loss on trade receivables can have on a company. The burden on the company increases, since more turnover must be generated to compensate for the loss. This is by no means self-evident, particularly for companies with a low profit margin: a company with a margin of 5% that loses income of 100,000 euros through debtor default must realise 2,000,000 euros of new business in order to compensate for this loss.

The premium payable for a credit insurance policy to protect against the risk of this loss is minimal in comparison.

TABLE 9.2 *Compensation in terms of higher turnover for unpaid debts, based on profit margin percentages*

Profit margin / Unpaid invoices	5%	10%	15%	20%
10,000	200,000	100,000	66,667	50,000
30,000	600,000	300,000	200,000	150,000
50,000	1,000,000	500,000	333,333	250,000
100,000	2,000,000	1,000,000	666,667	500,000
300,000	6,000,000	3,000,000	2,000,000	1,500,000
500,000	10,000,000	5,000,000	3,333,333	2,500,000
1,000,000	20,000,000	10,000,000	6,666,667	5,000,000

4 Interaction between working capital and company return

The primary objective of every company is the creation of shareholder value. Various factors can contribute towards the realisation of this objective. One of them is the efficient management of the working capital.

During the operating cycle, a company needs financial resources (working capital) in order to:

- ➔ purchase goods, raw materials and other necessary aids for production (inventory/stocks and orders in progress);
- ➔ transform raw materials, production aids, goods in processing and orders in progress into finished products;
- ➔ finance sales to customers who do not pay cash on delivery (trade receivables).

In part, the above-mentioned activities (and, by extension, the company assets) will be auto-financed by:

- ➔ making use of the payment periods granted by suppliers, which means that actual payment will be made later than delivery (trade debts);
- ➔ paying employees and other third parties only after they have performed their allotted tasks (other debts).

There is therefore a requirement for (net) working capital. Inventory, trade receivables and trade debts all play an important role – and credit insurance can have a crucial effect on these last two balance sheet items.

GOLDEN RULE

The key challenge for the effective management of working capital rests in the optimisation of what is known as the cash generation cycle; in other words, the manner and speed with which turnover is converted into liquid resources. For example, a period of time inevitably elapses between the purchase of raw materials and the conversion of those raw materials into cash receipts through the sale of finished products. By keeping the amount of working capital as low as possible and the cash generation cycle as short as possible, it is likely that a higher operational return will result.

In an extreme form, we can see this principle at work in the activities of the private equity funds, which acquire (family) companies through a leveraged buy-out (an LBO is usually accompanied by a high level of debt financing) as an investment. It is noticeable that one of their first actions is to drastically reduce the investment in working capital. In this manner, millions of euros of cash are freed up, which can be used to reduce levels of outstanding debt.

We will now outline the impact of working capital on the liquidity of a company. Then we will show how the efficient management of working capital can lead to better financial results and a higher return. Credit insurance can play an important role in both of these.

4.1 LIQUIDITY

In contrast to the longer-term focus of matters relating to company return, the question of liquidity is of more importance in the short term.

Credit management plays a crucial role in liquidity management, since outstanding trade receivables represent about 15 to 30 % of the balance sheet total. For most companies, this is a significant investment of resources.

→ *Net working capital (NWC)*

To assess the liquidity of a company, we must first look at its net working capital. Net working capital can be defined as (also see figure 9.2):

permanent capital (equity + long term debt) on the liabilities side – fixed assets
or
current assets – short-term debt (duration of less than 1 year).

This latter definition can also be defined more broadly:
(stocks + receivables of less than 1 year, including trade receivables + cash investments + liquid resources + accruals) – (financial debts of less than 1 year + trade debts with a duration up to 1 year + other non-interest-bearing debts).

In other words, the NWC shows the extent to which the financing of the fixed assets can be fully covered (or not) by the company's permanent capital (equity + long-term debt). The difference between the permanent capital and the fixed assets can be positive (liquidity > 1) or negative (liquidity < 1).

A positive NWC shows that the company is liquid in the broadest sense of the term (current ratio). This liquidity is important, since it indicates whether or not the company at the present moment is able to meet its short-term payment obligations.

A positive NWC equates to the margin of safety rule, often referred to as the 'golden rule of finance': every possession or item of property with a finite life or period of duration should be financed with financial resources that have the same period of duration. In other words, the financial resources must be organised to reflect the life expectancy of the investment.

FIGURE 9.2 *Position of the NWC in a company's financial structure*

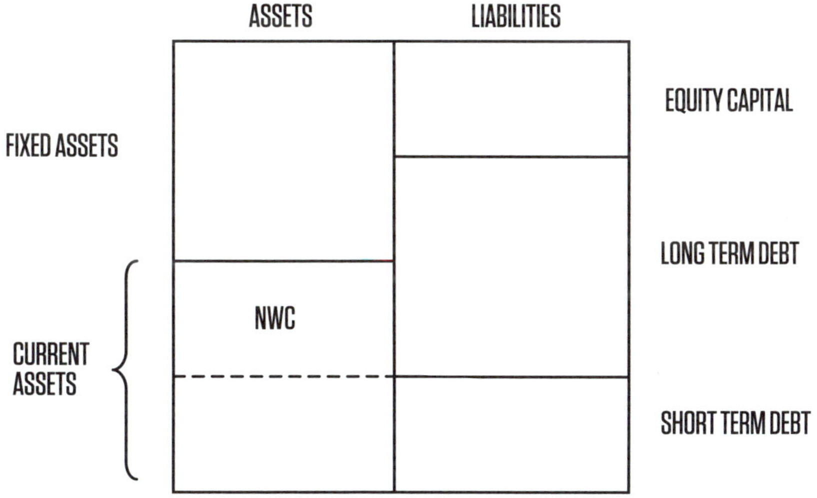

GOOD ADVICE

It is clear that credit insurance can make a contribution towards ensuring that this golden finance rule is maintained. If customers default on their payments (and one large insolvency can be enough), the amount of the unpaid debts can sometimes exceed the value of the positive NWC. In turn, your equity capital is negatively affected, as a result of which the level of permanent capital on the liabilities side of the balance sheet decreases.

→ *Working capital requirement (WCR)*

The key question is how large your net working capital needs to be. To determine this, it is first necessary to look more closely at your working capital requirement (WCR). A company's level of WCR will depend on its operational cycle: the purchase of raw materials, and the processing and sale of finished products. The WCR can be more or less defined as the amount of the inventory/ stocks and receivables (including customers) minus trade debts and other non-interest-bearing debts (tax, social insurance contributions, etc.). This definition can also be expressed in more detail:

(stocks + receivables of less than 1 year (including trade receivables) + accruals) – (trade debts + other short-term non-interest-bearing debts).

In every company there is a portion of the business activity that is funded instantly, almost as a matter of course. Most suppliers give credit through the payment dates on their invoices and staff are only paid at the end of the month. This instant financing tends to grow with the size of the company and can help in turn to finance a part of the company's own investment in customer credit and inventories.

The WCR is therefore the funding need that is necessary to implement the operating cycle. It is wise to keep this operational requirement for working capital as low as possible. In this way, the company only ties up a minimum amount of its financial resources in its basic, day-to-day business activities. There are three possible ways to reduce the level of WCR – and two of them are influenced by credit insurance:

1. reduce the number of days of customer credit: good credit management within the company, supported by a credit insurer, can make a huge difference;
2. increase the number of days of supplier credit: in this instance, the credit insurer can have an influence, if he fails to show trust in the company as a debtor; should this happen, the suppliers may well refuse to allow further payment deferment, insisting instead on cash payment;
3. reduce the average inventory period: this amounts to a faster rotation of stocks, by limiting them to just the essentials; this is primarily a logistical matter, on which credit insurance has little impact.

→ *Net treasury position*

Before we close this section on liquidity, it is important to look at the net treasury position. This can be defined as:
(cash investments + liquid resources) – short-term financial debts

This equates to the difference between NWC and WCR. This difference can either be positive or negative:

- → if the difference is positive, the company's liquidity situation is good;
- → if the difference is negative, the company needs to be careful; this is certainly the case if NWC < 0 and WCR > 0, which represents a very dangerous financial situation in the short term; the financial liquidity (cash investments and liquid resources) is lower than the level of outstanding financial debts in the short term, so that the company becomes dependent on the banks and other financiers for the continued implementation of its commercial activities.

Figure 9.3 illustrates a number of different situations, which can arise when analysing the net treasury aspect of liquidity, as it appears on a company's balance sheet:

FIGURE 9.3 *The net treasury position (source: Handbook of Financial Management, Intersentia, 2009)*

	NWC > 0	NWC < 0
WCR < 0	**Situation A** Very good	**Situation D** Good (if the net treasury is positive) **Situation E** Less good (if the net treasury is negative)
WCR > 0	**Situation B** Good (if the net treasury is positive) **Situation C** Less good (if the net treasury is negative)	**Situation F** Dangerous

Figure 9.3 also shows that there are intermediate positions, where each case or each sector must be viewed independently. With large distribution companies (such as Tesco, B&Q, Debenhams, Aldi, etc.) the WCR is always negative, since the customers pay in cash at the check-out (in other words, there are practically no trade receivables). This is combined with a very strict supply policy, where suppliers are expected to be able to respond quickly and flexibly to order needs *and* grant the supermarkets a payment period of 30 to 90 days. This means that the NWC can also be negative, but without any harmful effects for the liquidity of the company.

GOOD ADVICE

It is clear that good credit management, supported by credit insurance, can play an important role in maintaining the liquidity of the company by:

- preventing a positive NWC from becoming negative;
- by reducing WCR through the strict monitoring of outstanding trade receivables.

4.2 RETURN

→ *Principle*

Hopefully, the previous section will have shown that credit management can be an important part of the wider management of working capital within a company. A sound policy in this respect will not only improve liquidity (which is focussed on the short term), but also increase the company's overall profitability and return, thereby having a positive knock-on influence on both equity capital and solvency (which is more important in the long term).

Assets management on the basis of a correct approach to working capital can contribute in various ways towards the development and maintenance of a healthy financial structure:

- Effective assets management increases profitability, not only in terms of business profits but also in terms of the return on equity, since the unnecessary immobilisation of financial resources is eliminated. The reduction of assets in this manner implies a consequent reduction in financial costs, since all assets need to be financed. By achieving the same level of turnover through the use of a lower level of assets or a higher level of turnover without a concomitant increase in the use of assets, a company can approach the market with a more streamlined cost structure, which will allow either an increase in profit margins or greater price competitiveness.

- Restricting the level of assets goes hand in hand with restricting the level of liabilities – and nothing is for free on the liabilities side of the balance sheet. This can lead to benefits in terms of:
  - Obvious costs in respect of financial debts, as well as the remuneration due on the equity capital (the funding burden plus a risk premium translated into the payment of dividends);
  - Less obvious but nonetheless significant opportunity costs in respect of the credit granted by suppliers (interest on arrears, price subsidies, the costs of irrevocable and confirmed documentary credits, discounts for cash payment, etc.).

As previously mentioned, the trade receivables are the last step in the process, which transforms working resources into available resources (liquidity). In this context, debt management and, by extension, credit insurance can yield significant benefits in terms of wider assets management.

And what about the impact on profitability and overall returns? First, it is necessary to make a distinction between two different types of return:

- ROA (return on assets). This reflects the company's return on the use of its invested resources. Operational profitability is therefore the most important element of ROA. This is particularly useful from the perspective of the daily management of the company, since it shows whether the company is performing efficiently (or not). The emphasis is clearly on the company assets.
- ROE (return on equity). This is primarily of interest to the shareholders: what profit are they making on the use of their (money) capital. The accent here is on the company liabilities: the equity capital and the financial leverage effect are the key elements.

→ *Return on assets (ROA)*

ROA is the return on assets in their totality (including financial investments). It is also often referred to as the return on total investments. This indicates that the return is mainly the result of investment in assets and that liabilities in themselves do not generate return.

BE SMART

ROA is an instrument to realise ROE. By managing ROA effectively, it is possible to:

- keep liabilities in check;
- ensure that financial charges do not become too important in relation to the operating result.

We will now try to illustrate these points.

The return on total assets before tax (in %) is determined by the following formula:

$$\text{ROA} = \frac{\text{Result before tax}}{\text{Total assets}} \times 100$$

The return on total assets before tax therefore gives the global return on operational investments and financial investments, including extraordinary profits, and is independent of the method of financing (equity or debt). The result before tax on the turnover is the company's profit margin. The formula above can thus be converted (in %):

$$\text{ROA} = \frac{\text{Result before tax}}{\text{Turnover}} \times \frac{\text{Turnover}}{\text{Total assets}} \times 100$$

= profit margin x rotation total assets

The operational return on company assets (not including the fixed financial assets) is the most important element of this equation. A high rotation means that the company assets are being used wisely. This implies that the return will increase as the total on the balance sheet decreases, simply as a result of the faster rotation of the assets. The faster the rotation, the more frequently the profit margin per rotation can be realised.

It is therefore important to calculate the rotation factor (the speed of circulation) for each component part of the assets, since this is the only way to make a correct diagnosis of the overall situation and identify where possible problems caused by slow circulation may be occurring. To do this, use is often made of the so-called Du Pont de Nemours schedule (from the chemical company of the same name). For example, it may be interesting to further sub-divide the company assets in accordance with operational criteria rather than accounting criteria. With regard to trade receivables, this might mean 'trade receivables product A, product B, product C, etc.', perhaps further split into 'foreign customers/domestic customers', 'public sector/private sector', 'retail/wholesale', etc.

The worst situation for any company is a low (or falling) profit margin combined with a low (or falling) rotation of the company's working assets. If the circulation of the assets is too slow, more company assets are necessary to achieve the same level of turnover. This will increase the financial costs for the funding of these additional assets, while the share of equity in the financing of the assets can no longer follow, as a result of the shrinkage in operational profitability. This is a vicious circle that can only be broken by being as parsimonious as possible with the company's assets: this allows the company to reduce investments on the assets side of the balance sheet and free up capital sources within the company on the liabilities side of the balance sheet.

Here are two extreme examples to illustrate these points:

1 A steel company, as a production company, needs to invest heavily in operational assets: extensive infrastructure (buildings, machines), inventory of steel and other raw materials, etc. This limits the rotation of the operational assets, which must be compensated by a high profit margin based on a superior added value.

GOOD ADVICE

The result (profit/loss) before tax can be improved through efficient credit management in the following areas:

- → there will be fewer extraordinary losses as a result of unpaid trade receivables;
- → carefully monitoring will result in a lower amount of trade receivables on the assets side of the balance sheet, which in turn results in the faster rotation of these assets, so that the profit margin can be realised more frequently on an annual basis;
- → the lower amount of trade receivables in turn reduces the need for financing on the liabilities side of the balance sheet, with a knock-on benefit in terms of reduced interest payments; this will lead to a higher profit and return.

2 A discounter (such as Aldi) works with a very low profit margin: the sale prices are scarcely more than the purchase prices. Even so, company return remains high because of the fast rotation of the company's operational assets. The nature of their supermarkets limits their investment in fixed assets. Moreover, the number of brands on offer is also limited, which leads to lower stocks. The customers pay cash or with a debit card at the check-out, so that there are no outstanding trade accounts.

This higher profit can (after tax) be allocated to the equity capital of the company. And in view of the lower balance sheet total, this results in greater solvency (equity capital/total invested capital). This will increase the creditworthiness of the company with the banks, as well as improving its bank credit rating, which is important within the context of Basle II/Basle III (see later).

Credit insurance, as an important support instrument for the internal credit management of a company, must also be viewed from this same perspective.

→ *Return on equity (ROE)*

The return on equity before tax (in %) is determined by the following formula:

$$\text{ROA} = \frac{\text{Profit or loss for the financial year before tax}}{\text{Equity capital}} \text{ X } 100$$

The level of this shareholder return is largely influenced by two key factors: the return on (mainly operational) assets and the working of the financial leverage effect.

The financial leverage effect comes into operation when a company uses loans (i.e. debts) to finance its assets. This foreign capital from third parties is subject to financial charges, which must be borne by the company and which are independent of profit and loss. A company is only prepared to use this method of asset financing if the financial leverage effect is positive; in other words, if the return on the investment in assets is greater than the financial costs of the debts used to finance those assets. However, the financial leverage can also be negative, if the return on the investment in assets is lower than the financial costs of the initial loan. This was the experience of many companies during the financial and economic crisis of 2008-2009.

The financial leverage effect plays a role in the ROE formula, an effect that is dependent on two elements:

1 The comparison between the return on assets and the average interest costs on the borrowed capital;
2 The proportional relationship between debt and equity capital: the higher this is, the more powerfully the financial leverage works.

The private equity funds apply this latter factor with vigour when they acquire other assets (family companies) with often aggressive leveraged buy-out (LBO) financing. Leveraged buy-out is a specific type of acquisition, in which the takeover of the controlling interest in a company is made by using a significant amount of borrowed capital from banks and/or capital markets. Interest and principal repayments are usually made from the cash-flows of the acquired company (target), while the assets of the target typically serve as collateral for the borrowed capital. Since the debt normally has a lower cost of capital than the equity, the returns on the equity increase with increasing debt. The debt thus effectively serves as a *lever* to increase returns, which explains the origin of the term LBO. This practice was encouraged during the first decade of the new century by the very low rates of interest in the financial markets.

GOOD TO KNOW

To achieve a positive leverage effect, a company therefore needs to fund its activities with cheap debts, whose financial costs are significantly lower than the value of the benefits in terms of operational return. This also explains the importance of a low level of working capital requirement (WCR), with minimal levels of inventory, in combination with a minimal number of outstanding trade receivables on the assets side of the balance sheet and a maximal amount of trade debts and other non-interest-bearing debts (advance payments, tax, social insurance contributions, etc.) on the liabilities side. These operational debts, particularly the trade debts, are usually cheaper (and easier to arrange) than financial debts incurred with banks.

Within this context, credit insurance has a double role to play:
1 It keeps the number of outstanding trade receivables in check by a process of careful monitoring, working in conjunction with the insured party's own credit management team. This is linked to the financial function of credit insurance (see above).

2 It helps to maintain the supplier credit of a company through a positive response to the credit limit applications put forward by insured parties in respect of that company. This is linked to the economic function of credit insurance (see above).

This reflects neatly the double benefit of credit insurance: it can work to the advantage of companies and shareholders alike.

5 Credit insurance as an outsourcing instrument

Credit insurance needs to be seen in broader terms than the simple provision of default cover through the sale of a policy. It can also help companies to enlist outside sources of assistance that can provide valuable input to their credit management systems.

5.1 POSSIBILITIES FOR THE OUTSOURCING OF CREDIT MANAGEMENT FUNCTIONS

Table 9.3 shows the percentage of companies that carry out their own credit management internally and the percentage that outsource some parts of this function to external agencies.

This shows that the majority of companies still manage their credit management internally. Please note, however, that credit control is not the same thing as credit management: it is simply a part of it. Nevertheless, an increasing number of other credit functions are also being outsourced. This can either be on a one-off or a continuous basis, risk analysis being the most popular function for the use of this external approach. It is in the context of this kind of outsourcing that credit insurance can be of considerable use.

5.2 CREDIT INSURANCE IS A MANAGEMENT TOOL

Credit insurance is a management tool that allows the supplier to structure and support his credit policy. The insured party can benefit from four distinct services: screening of customers, the monitoring of customers, the collection of outstanding trade accounts and (when necessary) the payment of loss compensation. To assist in these tasks, the insured party can make use of the insurer's extensive database. This database contains financial information on companies (debtors) worldwide, offering the insured party access to numerous (commercial) market details, both at home and abroad. Euler Hermes, for example, has more than 40 million companies listed in its database.

TABLE 9.3 *Internal credit management and the outsourcing of credit management functions (source: Credit Management Research Centre, Leeds University Business School / Euler Hermes, 2006)*

	1	2	3	4	5
All countries	90	64	58	46	46
Belgium	87	46	58	40	46
France	78	46	36	73	73
Germany	82	71	39	13	21
Netherlands	97	50	67	50	38
Hungary	80	46	50	33	32
Italy	94	90	97	68	68
Spain	85	57	86	57	57
Poland	75	68	40	50	50
Portugal	97	96	92	89	94
UK	**98**	**85**	**72**	**46**	**46**

1 = % internal credit management 2 = % outsourcing risk analysis 3 = % outsourcing collection 4 = % outsourcing legal advice 5 = % outsourcing recovery

HOW IT WORKS

The insured supplier therefore saves costs on the acquisition of financial information (for which he would otherwise have to pay), and saves time and energy that he would otherwise need to invest in the analysis and monitoring of his buyer risks, and the chasing of his payment delays. This increases also the pressure exerted by the insurer on his debtor and enhances the likelihood that the debts will be settled on time.

5.3 OUTSOURCING CREDIT MANAGEMENT FUNCTIONS THROUGH CREDIT INSURANCE

In 2006, the Credit Management Research Centre of the Leeds University Business School made a study of credit management in Europe and the possible impact of credit insurance as an instrument of outsourcing. The study was commissioned by Euler Hermes. More than 2,000 different companies in various countries were interviewed. The sample was representative of the sector in terms of size, scale and activity.

As far as we know, this was the first study of its kind in this field. A distinction was made between companies that were credit insured and companies that were not. 51% of the companies surveyed had a policy. Of these, 63% related to cover for default risk both at home and abroad, with a further 25% exclusively for foreign default and just 12% exclusively for domestic default.

→ *Stakeholders*

The survey reached a number of noteworthy conclusions with regard to the positive impact of credit insurance on the relations of the insured party with his suppliers, customers and the banks. The results confirmed that credit insurance, as a tool for the support of credit management, considerably enhances the relationship of the insured party with each of these key stakeholders.

→ *Relationships with suppliers*

Suppliers regard credit insured companies as being better credit risks, since their policy protects them against the negative domino-effect that can be created by bad debts.

Table 9.4 shows that in general credit insured companies are able to secure more favourable standard payment conditions than uninsured companies: an average of 50 days against 41 days, which results in a positive effect on their cash-flow of 9 days. The study also revealed that 90% of the insured companies were able to secure trade credit with their suppliers, against a figure of just 73% for the uninsured. In other words, there is a significantly larger access to trade credit for companies with their own credit insurance policy.

If we look at the total effective credit period (the official payment period plus any additional deferment), the cash-flow benefit is reduced to 7 days. This is because non-insured companies are more likely in relative terms to have longer periods of additional deferment than their insured counterparts.

TABLE 9.4 *Elements that determine relations with suppliers (source: Credit Management Research Centre, University of Leeds Business School / Euler Hermes)*

	Credit insured	Uninsured	Potential impact
Standard credit conditions offered by the suppliers (in days)	50	41	+ 9 days cash-flow
% of companies that secure trade credit from their suppliers	90	73	N/A
Total number of credit days	54	47	+ 7 days cash-flow
% of companies that obtain preferential credit conditions from the suppliers	69	58	N/A
% of discount that the suppliers offer for cash payment	3.4	2.5	-0.9% of the transaction value
% of suppliers that offer a discount for cash payment	25	23	N/A

All these elements result in preferential credit conditions being granted by suppliers to 69% of their credit insured debtors, as opposed to just 58% of their other customers. In this context, however, it should be noted that the suppliers tend to look first at the size of the customer and the length of the commercial relationship when making their credit decisions.

As far as discounts for cash payment is concerned, suppliers grant this to a much smaller degree: discounts are only offered in about 25% of cases, with there being little difference between the insured and the uninsured. This confirms what was said earlier in this chapter – discounts for cash payment can sometimes be very expensive, when viewed from the supplier's perspective. In cases where discounts are offered, the insured customers get a higher average discount of 0.9% on the basis of transaction value.

On the other side of the coin, it should also be noted that the customer's choice of supplier is not in the first instance determined by the supplier's willingness to grant trade credit. The most important factors include:

- the reliability of the supplier;
- the quality of his products and services;
- the speed of delivery, once an order has been placed;
- the cost of the product or service.

Suppliers are extremely important for the insured party, since a company's external purchases represent on average between 50 and 60% of its total expenditure. This means that a saving of just 5% on external purchases can actually increase profits by 30%. In other words, there is an important leverage effect at play, so that a marginal reduction in external costs can generate a significant percentage increase in the company's overall results. And the trade credit granted by the supplier is an important factor in this respect.

→ *Relationships with the banks*

In recent years companies have been increasingly confronted with the restrictive lending practices of the banks. This attitude was initially encouraged by the introduction of the Basle II regulations, but was significantly enhanced by the financial and economic crisis of 2008-2009. Depending upon a company's level of reliance on short-term credit financing, the efficient management of working capital (and, in particular, the number of trade receivables on the assets side of the balance sheet) is crucial for the prosperity, growth and survival chances of that company. Companies that do not monitor and control the trade credit they have granted to their customers, with its resulting implications for cash-flow, are simply jeopardising their chances for growth and increasing the likelihood of insolvency.

In table 9.5 we can see that insured companies in general have a longer relationship with their banks and are also able to obtain credit facilities more easily. This is a sign of confidence and trust.

Credit insured companies therefore have a lower requirement for short-term financing, even though the banks are actually more prepared to lend them money. Table 9.6 confirms this tendency:

- In the short-term, credit insured companies make more use of non-guaranteed overdraft facilities, whereas non-insured companies are more likely to

TABLE 9.5 *Elements that determine relations with banks (source: Credit Management Research Centre, University of Leeds Business School / Euler Hermes)*

	Credit insured	Uninsured
Average number of years of the relationship with the current bank	21	16
% of companies that during the last 5 years were granted financial assistance on the basis of the current capital structure	50	44
% of companies that were granted a bank loan during the previous year	49	34
Average rate of interest for a bank loan %	3.50	3.95

WHAT YOU NEED TO KNOW

It is important to realise that credit insurance can lead to cheaper credit conditions from banks and other financiers (on average, 0.45% lower rates of interest). The underlying philosophy is clear: the support offered by credit insurance leads to the better management of both debt risks (credit management) and the working capital. This in turn results in positive effects on the balance sheet ratios (for example, higher levels of solvency with the same level of equity capital). Because there are fewer outstanding trade receivables, there is also a reduced requirement for short-term credit, which in turn reduces interest charges and increases overall return. If the profit remains within the company, this boosts the level of the equity capital still further, encouraging the banks to give the company a higher internal rating within the framework of the Basle II/III regulations and resulting at the same time in a reduced need to make use of the banks' own equity capital, ensuring lower capital costs for the remaining credits granted by the bank and a lower interest margin for the insured party.

use (or be obliged to use) straight loans: fixed short-term advances, mostly with guarantees.

- As far as long-term guaranteed credit is concerned, insured companies have more and better opportunities to finance their investments over a long period.
- Insured companies can issue more commercial paper, which indicates that their higher credit rating makes it easier for them to attract offers from the public market when they need to acquire short-term resources.
- Insured companies have greater opportunities to make use of factoring. Factoring is a form of asset-based financing, whereby outstanding trade receivables are used to attract cash resources. Factoring is often used by banks, to give companies in trouble a final injection of funding (although this is not the only purpose of factoring). The great risk with factoring is the possibility of fraud: the factoring customer can offer fictitious, non-existent invoices in the hope of gaining new and desperately needed resources. For this reason, the factoring company must have great confidence in the customer before they enter into a factoring agreement.
- Extended trade credit is also granted more easily to insured companies; this means that banks are more likely to agree a complementary short-term financing on the expiry date of the existing trade credit.

→ *Relationships with customers*

In a fast-moving and ever-changing world, where made-to-measure customer orientation and marketing are increasingly seen as the keys to success, trade credit and its associated benefits in terms of effective credit management can play an important role in ensuring the smooth development and maintenance of the relationship between supplier and customer. In other words, credit insurance can greatly assist the insured party's customer relationship management (CRM). By providing active support in this key area, the insurer allows the insured party to follow a dynamic policy of risk monitoring and control.

The study showed that 84% of credit insured companies regard the relationship with their customers as being vital, against just 79% of the non-insured companies.

The customer focus of insured companies is also reflected in table 9.7: in relative terms, the insured companies have a larger number of customers with credit limits, they receive more credit limit applications, and more of these applications are approved. The back-up provided by the credit insurer, by granting access to his extensive database, is a key factor in explaining these figures.

TABLE 9.6 *Access to financing (source: Credit Management Research Centre, Leeds University Business School / Euler Hermes, 2006)*

In %	Credit insured	Uninsured
Overdraft facilities with a bank	**62**	55
Guaranteed bank loans (short term)	30	42
Guaranteed bank loans (long term)	**49**	34
Leasing/hire-purchase	47	47
Commercial mortgages	15	15
Commercial paper	10	3
Factoring	**24**	5
Extended commercial credit	**41**	16
Venture capital	7	3
Group financing	34	33

This same support allows the insured companies to follow a more dynamic foreign trade policy: they export a greater proportion of their turnover to a greater number of overseas countries (an average of 30% against 24% for uninsured companies).

And a similar dynamism is evident in their innovation skills: their better overall organisation (which in part is the result of high-performance credit management systems) allows them to bring more new products and services onto the market than their non-insured colleagues.

TABLE 9.7 *Elements that determine relations with customers (source: Credit Management Research Centre, University of Leeds Business School / Euler Hermes)*

	Credit insured	Uninsured	Potential impact
% of customers with a credit limit	77	62	15% more customers with a credit limit
Number of credit applications received	1416	656	More credit applications each year
% of credit applications accepted	81	72	9% more accepted credit applications
% of turnover exported abroad	30	24	6% more sales exported
Average number of countries where exports are sent	6	3	Greater international market penetration
% of companies that introduce new products or services	64	57	Greater likelihood of launching new products/services
Number of customer accounts as a percentage of sales	0.83	0.34	Higher % of customer accounts in relation to sales

A good customer focus is clearly evident in the number of customer accounts as a percentage of turnover. The study also showed that insured companies have better long-term relations with their customers: 73% of them have repeat business, as opposed to just 67% of non-insured companies. This is a logical result: if suppliers are covered against default risks by credit insurance, they will be more easily prepared to do business time after time with the same customers. It is a sign that they are regarded as creditworthy. And even if the worst does happen and a customer fails, they are still insured against any loss incurred in respect of unpaid trade debts.

GOOD TO KNOW

This shows that credit insured companies have more customers with whom they build up a long-term relationship. This is very important. By creating a customer portfolio with a long-term perspective (in other words, reliable customers with the intention of making repeat purchases over a number of years), companies can develop a marketing policy for the medium to long term, instead of just the short term. This nearly always brings higher returns: a company that succeeds in retaining 5% more of its customers will normally see its profits rise by a minimum of 25%.

A good example of the above policy in practice is a company that develops a sales network on the basis of exclusive dealers. A change of dealer costs the company a great deal of money (training, assistance with marketing investments, etc.). For this reason, the key to success is the careful selection of dealers, which implies that the dealers must have sufficient financial resilience to withstand the occasional setbacks that every market throws up. The credit insurer can use his expertise to help the insured party with his selection process and with subsequent monitoring.

Credit insured companies are also more proactive in their willingness to adjust their credit conditions for specific reasons. They show more flexibility in:

- attracting new customers in general (30% against 19% for uninsured companies);
- beating the competition (32% against 17%);
- attracting large customers (56% against 50%).
- reacting to changes in customer risk (45% against 34%);
- responding to changes in economic circumstances (30% against 18%).

In a similar vein, 54% of credit insured companies see the granting of credit limits not as a purely financial transaction, but also as a marketing decision. The comparable figure for non-insured companies is just 28%.

However, it must again be emphasised that the granting of trade credit is only a secondary reason for a customer to choose a particular supplier: price, reliability and quality are all more important factors (see above).

CONCLUSION

Many diverse and varied factors can influence the decision to take out a credit insurance policy, as shown in figure 9.4.

FIGURE 9.4 *Flow chart of signals and influencing factors that highlight a need for credit insurance (source: Euler Hermes).*

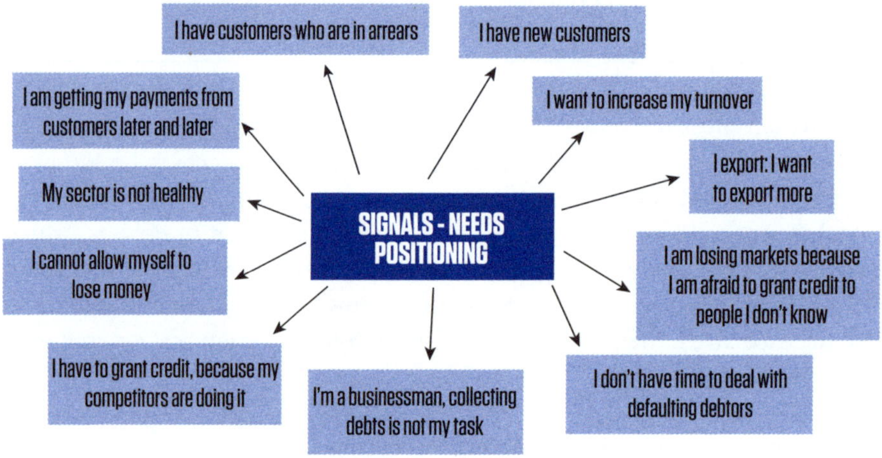

6 Synthesis of the financial impact of credit insurance

6.1 HOW GREAT IS THE FINANCIAL BENEFIT?

According to the study by the University of Leeds, all the above-mentioned factors have a significant financial impact. However, we can offer no real explanation for the level of nominal differences between insured companies and uninsured companies. Even so, these differences are spectacular, particularly if we realise that 74% of the non-insured companies gave cost price as their main reason for not having credit insurance:

- → With regard to turnover, insured companies enjoy a saving of 2.16% in comparison with their uninsured counterparts. On a turnover of 10,000,000 euros, this represents a saving of 216,000 euros. The largest portion (1.38%) is attributable to lower operational costs for the credit control department (for example, information gathering).

- In terms of interest costs, the saving is 0.45% (see section 5.3 of this chapter).

These figures become even more spectacular if we consider that the credit insurance premium is usually between 0.1% and 1% of the total insured turnover. One explanation might be that 63% of the companies questioned in the study had a turnover of less than 1,000,000 euros. These were nearly all family businesses, which have very little knowledge or experience of credit management. If some of these companies are credit insured, this usually means that they are compelled to monitor their outstanding trade receivables more closely. If they fail to do this, they risk losing their cover.

The margin of 2.16% on turnover for credit insured parties (leaving aside the 0.45% in respect of interest payments) broadly agrees with the study carried out by Intrum Justitia in 2012, which concluded that companies in Europe, on average, write off 2.8 % of their total receivables, reaching the unprecedented level of 340 billion euros.

6.2 PREMIUM COSTS VIEWED FROM A DIFFERENT PERSPECTIVE

MISUNDERSTANDING

The return on a credit insurance policy for an insured party should not be calculated by comparing at the end of each year the amount of premium paid with the amount of loss compensation received.

Whatever we might think of the nominal results, they at least show that credit insurance should not simply be regarded as cover against the possibility of bad debts. A company that uses this service as a *passe partout* is missing the opportunity to optimise its performance in several fields. Nevertheless, we must recognise that the temptation is there for some companies to regard credit insurance as nothing more than a license to sell and as a means of claiming compensation if things go wrong. This is a very short-sighted view. The analysis of existing customers or prospects is a powerful preventative factor that reduces the cost, weight and frequency of default-only credit insurance. The better credit insurers and advisers do more than insure risk and pay out compensation: they are experts in credit risk assessment and management, and feed invaluable intelligence into trade-related operations.

For this reason, the credit insurance premium must be viewed from a broader perspective:

- *Sensu stricto*: it covers the loss on defaulted trade debts;
- *Sensu lato*: it optimises the management of working capital and assists in effective credit management; the credit insurance policy must be viewed first and foremost as a management instrument that results in a better balance sheet structure; in this way – and perhaps most importantly – it also contributes towards the creation of added (shareholder) value in the company.

The banks will usually give a better internal credit rating to a credit insured company, which leads to a number of useful benefits:
- the banks will be inclined to lend credit more easily;
- the credit costs (interests margins) will be lower, which in turn increases the profitability of the company.

Finally, it must be noted that, within the wider insurance sector, the credit insurance branch is regarded by European legislators as being the most risk-intensive branch. This is reflected in the higher technical provisions to which credit insurance is subject and the higher reserves that the insurers need to set aside, in comparison with other branches. And higher risks mean higher premiums – a fact that is all too easily overlooked by many companies.

CHAPTER 10
THE ECONOMIC IMPORTANCE OF CREDIT INSURANCE

Because of the key contribution made by credit insurance in the management of working capital, it also has a major economic impact. As a result of the product's clear position in supporting supplier trade credit, the credit insurer almost acts as a kind of invisible bank. In this respect, we have recently seen several examples in our newspapers of failing high-street chains, each stressing the lack of supplier credit as a major reason for their inability to carry on business. Indeed, in some instances there has even been the suggestion that it was the lack of credit insurance that caused this situation. However, as we have seen from earlier chapters in this book, credit insurance is actually a trade enabler, which is closely linked to the real economy. In fact, it is right in the middle of it!

WHAT YOU NEED TO KNOW

The economic importance of credit insurance makes itself felt in many areas. It is sometimes even said that credit insurance is of strategic importance for the healthy life of a country's economy. This became clear during the financial and economic crisis of 2008-2009. Under the supervision of the European Union, a number of countries introduced temporary top-up cover backed by state guarantee, when private credit insurance only partially accepted new credit limit requests or reduced existing cover.

1 Macro-economic impact

1.1 ANTI-DOMINO EFFECT

Credit insurance increases economic stability by absorbing losses that otherwise would need to be borne by the insured party, with all the negative economic consequences this implies. Credit insurance eliminates the negative spill-over effect that major insolvencies can have on the supplier's network. An insolvency can also have indirect consequences. The company most directly concerned not only loses an important part (perhaps all) of the money it was owed by the defaulting debtor, but as a result also finds it more difficult to pay what it owes to other suppliers. When this happens, these other suppliers might also find themselves in cash-flow difficulties – and so the problem spreads.

One of the best examples of this scenario is also one of the oldest. At the end of the 1960s, the original Rolls Royce Motor Company unexpectedly went bust in the UK. One of its major suppliers, a public company, was immediately seen to be a victim of the crash, being saddled with a huge unpaid debt that threatened its own solvency position. Its shares fell on the stock exchange and suppliers, in turn, started to withdraw credit terms. However, with the permission of its credit insurer (not Euler Hermes, in this instance!), a press statement was released, confirming that credit insurance cover was held by the company, which therefore had every expectation of claims being met for all of its outstandings. Lo and behold, suppliers resumed deliveries on credit terms – and the share price rose to levels even higher than before Rolls Royce crashed!

The chance that an important supplier is dragged down by the insolvency of one of his customers is much smaller when his outstanding trade accounts are covered by credit insurance. This applies *a priori* to other suppliers further along the economic chain.

1.2 MULTIPLIER EFFECT

GOOD TO KNOW

Credit insurance supports both domestic and foreign trade by making it possible to undertake transactions that would otherwise involve too much risk – and therefore could not be carried out. In this respect, credit insurance contributes towards economic growth. Trade credit is an integral part of economic life.

When a credit insurer approves the large majority of the credit applications he receives, thereby providing his insured customers (who are suppliers) with default cover, he is facilitating the smooth running of the relations between the different commercial partners. This helps to stimulate global economic activity.

This argument was recently confirmed by the Dutch Central Bank, which conducted a study in 2010 that showed that credit insurance had a positive multiplier effect of 2.3 on international trade. In other words, every euro covered by a credit insurer leads to a growth of 2.3 euros in international trade.

Does this mean that the credit insurer can also have the opposite effect, if he decides to adopt a more restrictive policy? During the crisis of 2008-2009 the insurers were often criticised that their attitude was pro-cyclic and not counter-cyclic. The role of the credit insurer is to facilitate trade transactions. He accepts default risks in return for the payment of a premium. However, some risks are simply too great in relation to the amount of the premium paid by the insured company. When this happens, there are two possible options:

1. the level of the premium is increased to such an extent that the supplier's profit margin is almost completely eroded;
2. the level of cover is reduced or withdrawn entirely.

FOOD FOR THOUGHT

If credit insurers had a clear counter-cyclic approach, this would mean that they would continue to accept all risks, even the ones that are virtually impossible to cover. The insured parties would then be required to pay for this 'policy' through a massive increase in premiums, which works, in particular, to the disadvantage of companies with a relatively healthy debt portfolio. In insurance, everything stands or falls with the mutualisation of risks.

2 Mirror of the economic cycle

The economy has always been characterised by a succession of cycles: bad times are followed by good times, and vice versa. By now, it should be evident that credit insurance, by the very nature of its core task – the provision of cover for the trade receivables of the insured party against the risk of insolvency on the part of his debtor – is sensitive to the changes brought about by these cycles. In periods of economic decline, the loss ratio (the proportional relationship between loss claims paid out and premiums received) will increase.

Fortunately, the credit insurer has at his disposal a kind of internal alarm bell, which allows him to anticipate these developments. He is in a perfect position to develop his own barometer of the economic cycle – a tool that is wholly compatible with his role as a global credit manager. His database contains masses of structured information that can be used to predict changes in the economic cycle. For example:

- In a positive sense: an increase in the number of credit limit applications is a sign that the economy is picking up. It reflects an increase in economic activity. The same is true if the average amount of credit requested per application also increases.
- In a negative sense: an increase in the number of requests for the extension of debtor payment dates or an increase in the number of submitted loss claims is usually a signal that there are difficult days ahead for the economy. Both phenomena suggest increasing liquidity problems. This usually goes hand in hand with a more restrictive approach on the part of the insurer (with more reductions or even terminations of existing credit limits).

3 The invisible bank

→ *Principle*

Covering trade receivables is just one side of the credit insurance coin. The granting of a credit limit by one company means the creation of a supplier debt at another company. When the credit insurer acts restrictively against a particular debtor company, the suppliers of that company will insist on a shorter payment period, perhaps even cash payment.

As a consequence, the working capital requirement (WCR) will increase at the debtor company, leading to a more difficult liquidity situation.

WHAT YOU NEED TO KNOW

For this reason, the credit insurer has enormous (economic) importance for the funding cycle of a company. This importance has increased in recent years through the consolidation of the sector. When a branch office of one of the three major credit insurance groups acts restrictively in respect of a local debtor, it is likely (in principle, at least) that the restriction will apply throughout the group worldwide – not just in the home country.

In the past, it was possible for the debtor company in question to turn to suppliers in other countries, where the local credit insurer might not be so well informed or so critical. Sectoral consolidation has changed all this. Nowadays, the negative opinion of a credit insurer spreads quickly throughout the market.

FOOD FOR THOUGHT

The key position of the credit insurer is not always easily accepted by the various operators in the financial markets (including the financial institutions).

In this capacity, it is possible to say that the credit insurers function as a kind of invisible bank, even though they are not directly involved in cash funding. A negative attitude from a credit insurer may lead indirectly to a reduction in the level of supplier credit granted by the sellers of goods and services.

→ *Practical example*

TABLE 10.1 *Balance sheet of company X in euros*

ASSETS		LIABILITIES	
Fixed assets		**Equity capital**	
Buildings	3,000,000	Capital + reserves	1,500,000
Machines	1,500,000	**Long-term financing**	
Financial assets	950,000	Bank	2,000,000
Current assets		**Short-term financing**	
Stock/inventory	1,500,000	Bank	3,500,000
Trade receivables	3,000,000	Suppliers (trade debts)	2,500,000
Cash	50,000	Other (tax, soc. ins.)	500,000
TOTAL	10,000,000		10,000,000

In table 10.1, debts to suppliers make up 25% of the balance sheet total.

Company X makes an accounting loss of 1.5 million euros in the financial year N-1. The non-cash write-offs are lower than this amount, so that the company is forced to use its cash resources to keep its operating cycle going. In other words, there is a cash drain. If this happens again the following year, its equity capital will gradually disappear.

There is also a problem with the company's liquidity: the fixed assets (5,450,000 euros) are only partially financed (3,500,000 euros) through liabilities (equity capital + long-term bank loans) that do not expire within the next 12 months. The remainder of the funding consists of short-term financing, including outstanding debts to suppliers.

Through the cover he provides to his insured customer, the supplier of company X, the credit insurer is faced with a potential loss risk of 2,500,000 euros. Because company X seems to be in difficulties, it is important for the credit insurer to monitor the situation closely. To do this, he needs information that comes directly from company X itself. The supplier company that is insured by the credit insurer can help in this matter by providing details about the balance sheet, profit and loss account and existing bank credits.

If the credit insurer does not receive this information, he will not be able to review or monitor his risk properly and will (probably) be forced to reduce the credit limit on company X, or even cancel it; whereas if proper and relevant information had been received, it is possible (or even likely) that a negative decision would not have been necessary. Once a negative decision has been made, this may have resulted in other suppliers of company X reducing their payment periods, or even demanding cash payment for future deliveries. Applied to the balance sheet shown above, this might mean:

- that the payment period is halved (for example, from 60 days to 30 days), so that the supplier credit is reduced to 1,250,000 euros;
- that, in the worst instance, suppliers demand cash payment, so that trade debts disappear completely from the liabilities side of the balance sheet.

Consequently, company X needs to go in urgent search of new sources of funding, assuming that its assets do not otherwise decrease. This funding might come from a bank or a factoring company, on the basis of company X's own outstanding trade receivables assets. Nevertheless, in view of the difficulties that it is currently facing, it will not be easy for the company to find new lenders and any new credit will certainly be more expensive than the supplier credit it has enjoyed in the past (which, in principle, is 'free', if we ignore the opportunity costs associated with the non-utilisation of possible discounts for cash payment).

Let us assume that company X is able to secure additional cash facilities of 2.5 million euros at a rate of interest of 5% per annum. This means the additional payment of 125,000 euros in interest each year.

If no alternative to supplier credit can be found, company X will soon find itself with acute liquidity problems. Its working capital (stocks/inventory and trade receivables) and the operational cycle linked with it, will both suffer from lack of adequate funding. And once the activities of the company can no longer be financed, a declaration of insolvency is the only way out.

4 The representative of the suppliers

When a debtor gets into difficulties, the supplier is often left to sort out the problem on his own. The credit insurer is concerned with the best interests of the supplier company and throws his weight behind him, in the hope of being able to rescue something from the situation. The credit insurer therefore acts to defend the interests of the supplier. To do this, he will involve all other suppliers of the same defaulting company, who are also insured with him.

The difficulty and delicacy of this task should not be underestimated. In cases of insolvency, the banks are generally in a stronger position, because of the securities they hold, and can therefore take a harder line. For example, they might have mortgages on the fixed assets of the debtor, whereas the supplier is often left standing in the cold.

It is interesting to note that this joining of supplier forces to apply greater pressure in potential insolvency situations is something that has developed almost automatically over time, under the impulse of the market.

The position of the credit insurer, as a representative and supporter of the supplier, is yet another factor that has been enhanced in recent years by the consolidation of the credit insurance market. In the past, a debtor company with liquidity problems, which had suppliers in several different countries, had to deal indirectly with a different credit insurer in each country. The consolidation of the market has reduced the number of credit insurers and incorporated them into three large credit insurance groups. The debtor now deals in general with any of the three major groups, which represent as insurer the suppliers from the different countries involved, because the insurance cover provided by the groups now extends to all suppliers worldwide. This creates a much better negotiating position:

- a company that fails to settle its debts on time can often be 'persuaded' to pay, if it does not want its credit limit to be reduced or revoked by the credit insurer;
- in the event of an insolvency, the suppliers with credit insurance stand in a stronger position vis à vis the receiver/administrator.

FOOD FOR THOUGHT

It is often better if the credit insurer acts as a third party representative on behalf of the suppliers. The suppliers often have business and emotional ties with their debtors stretching back over many years, which can sometimes hinder a rational and objective approach to the measures that need to be taken in the best interests of the supplier companies.

5 The gamekeeper and shock-absorber of the economy

Debtors who get into difficulties, for whatever reason, will usually be confronted by a restrictive attitude on the part of the credit insurer, whose first objective is to prevent/minimise loss. Nevertheless, there will usually be consultation between the credit insurer and the debtor company, in addition to the discussions that the debtor will inevitably have with other interested parties (such as the banks).

In most cases, the debtor will already have adjusted his approach and taken necessary measures to (hopefully) turn the tide of his fortunes. If this is not the case, the consultation process with the credit insurer may result in the debtor being forced to change his methods and actions. Should he fail to do so, he risks losing the confidence of the credit insurer.

In this sense, it is possible to speak of credit insurers as being the 'gamekeepers' of the economy. They detect the threats, cyclical trends and other winds of change that impact the financial health of the companies in their care, and, by applying pressure to the funding cycle of their working capital, persuade them to alter any behavioural bad habits. And when losses, however unexpected, do actually occur, they are also there to act as 'shock-absorbers', limiting the damaging effects to the economy as a whole.

ATTENTION!

It is crucial throughout this corrective process that the debtor possesses and displays 'normal' standards of business morality. Companies that deliberately allow their (mostly foreign) subsidiaries to go insolvent will instantly lose the confidence of the credit insurer.

6 Confirmation of the economic impact of credit insurance during the recent crisis

The financial and economic crisis of 2008-2009 was an extremely difficult period for the credit insurance sector. Several banks nearly went under. Several more had to be rescued by state intervention or takeover, and most of the rest were faced with acute financing problems, since the inter-banking market had all but ceased to function. (Even now, four to five years later, the banks are still not keen on adding new additional risks to their books by taking on more lending.) There was growing distrust in the real economy, as a result of which company turnover declined rapidly. In consequence, many companies were no longer able to cover their fixed costs and many experienced serious cash drains. The knock-on effect was major liquidity and cash-flow difficulties.

During the crisis, credit insurers were faced with this fast-growing problem, and found that the speed of events overtook the information they held on companies, effectively making it worthless (or, at least, inadequate). They found it increasingly difficult to establish which companies were still liquid and which were not. In these circumstances, the insurers felt that they had no choice but to adopt a restrictive credit approach.

It was in this context that several European governments introduced a number of crisis measures designed to support the credit insurance sector. The most important of these was the issuing of supplementary insurance with state guarantee (a kind of top-up cover), under the supervision of the European Commission. This was only a temporary measure, because in the long term it was not compatible with the principles of the free market in the European Union.

The measure was introduced at the instigation of the business community. The system was first applied in France at the end of 2008, and was called CAP. CAP stands for *Complément d'Assurance-crédit Public* (Supplementary Public Credit Insurance) and the same concept was adopted in several countries around this time.

The principle was that the state was ready to offer complementary insurance cover when the private credit insurer was reluctant to accept the full amount of the credit limit request on a particular buyer, or when that limit was reduced afterwards. In some countries government agencies even went so far as to offer additional coverage for the very worst risks, when the private credit insurer had completely refused or fully withdrawn its cover. However, this was the exception rather than the rule.

Within this context, in 2009 the UK government set up a short-term £5 billion Trade Credit Top-up Emergency Fund. However, this fund was later considered to be a failure, since the level of take-up was very low. There were two main explanations for this:

- the system was administratively complex and time-consuming, particularly for the insured party;
- it was also expensive.

But the system showed clearly that private credit insurance has an important influence on the liquidity position of companies and the economy in general.

FOOD FOR THOUGHT

For all its limitations, the European 'top-up cover' system represents an important milestone for the credit insurance sector. It was the first time that the private credit insurers entered into an alliance (however tentative) with the state. It remains to be seen how this alliance might be institutionalised in the future, but it may offer the sector an alternative to reinsurance. Having said this, it would undoubtedly be better if arrangements of this kind were to be made at a European level.

This 'top-up cover' system can be regarded as an experiment in co-insurance, a practice with which the private credit insurance sector – in contrast to its public counterpart – has had little experience to date.

PART 5

Limiting the risk

In chapters 11 and 12 we explain the two methods used by credit insurers to limit the potential risks they face:

1. *By linking the granting of credit limits to a system of guarantees and other remedies.*
2. *Through reinsurance.*

CHAPTER 11
THE CREDIT INSURER AND OTHER SECURITIES

In this chapter we will be dealing with the elements of possible security that the credit insurer can build into his system and from which he and the insured party can both benefit. These elements are fairly limited.

In a recent study of creditors in the Netherlands 84% of the suppliers questioned said that in the event of an insolvency they are usually left to their own devices, with little chance of recovering their unpaid claims. There is only one type of security that is valued by suppliers – and that is the retention of property/ownership rights over the goods that have been the subject of the sale. This is otherwise known as retention of title.

1 General

When a debtor goes bust, a creditor with outstanding trade receivables is usually an unsecured or non-privileged creditor. This means that the claims of all other preferred creditors must be settled before his claims can be considered, by which time most (if not all) of the debtor's available funds have been allocated to others. (In Belgium, for example, unsecured creditors recover on average just 1 to 3% of their outstanding claims).

One reason for this problem is that the creditor wants to do business with the debtor, and so does not wish to jeopardise their commercial relationship by asking for additional security. This is also one of the key reasons why many creditors/suppliers take out a credit insurance policy.

However, it may also be the case that where the buyer's bank has a fixed and floating charge over all the assets of the company (as security for its own lending), any such additional security will be of little value, in the face of the bank's prior claim.

Nevertheless, the provision of additional security may occasionally be agreed between creditor and debtor. This usually takes one of the following forms:

- retention of title;
- a surety given by the company's owners, the parent company or some other third party;
- a bank guarantee, payable at first request;
- a debt agreement or some other form of compensation for outstanding claims and debts.

Credit insurers sometimes make use of the retention of ownership/property rights. Obviously, if the goods that are the subject of a sale lose their identity when going through the buyer's handling or manufacturing process (for example, flour that is turned into bread), this is not feasible. However, if the goods remain clearly identifiable (for example, machine tools), this might be a practical option. Another option, rarely used, is when a credit insurer might ask for a guarantee of payment (for example, from a parent company).

Even so, there is no question of real securities on assets (as might be secured, for example, through a mortgage or a fixed and floating charge over all the assets). This type of guarantee is usually reserved as cover for longer term credit transactions.

The credit insurer can claim the benefit of any security of whatever kind granted to the creditor/supplier, since the rights over these securities (and their recovery) pass to the credit insurer as soon as he has paid out loss compensation to the creditor/supplier under the terms of the credit insurance policy.

WHAT YOU NEED TO KNOW

This is one of the reasons why the credit insurer prefers that any security of whatever kind, given by the debtor, is made directly to the benefit of the creditor, and not to the credit insurer. The creditor and the debtor have a clear commercial and contractual relationship with each other, which is not the case with the credit insurer. Any guarantee or other security structure is legally strengthened when it is issued by the buyer to a seller with whom he has signed a contract.

When a credit insurer demands security before he is prepared to approve a credit application from one of his insured parties, the insured party must obtain this security; otherwise his risk cover for the customer/debtor in question will not be valid. This is the clear responsibility of the insured customer, although the insurer will obviously provide his client with all necessary assistance and guidance.

2 Retention of title

Retention of title clauses are often seen as a natural extension of the credit economy; where suppliers are expected to sell goods on credit, there is a reasonable expectation that if they are not paid they should be able to repossess the goods. Nonetheless, in a number of jurisdictions local insolvency regimes or credit arrangement regimes prevent retention of title clauses from being enforced.

2.1 DEFINITION

Retention of ownership/property is a contractual agreement whereby the seller of goods stipulates that title in those goods will only be transferred to the buyer when he has completed his contractual obligations in full; in other words, when the agreed purchase price has been paid in full. If the buyer does not pay in full, the seller can demand the return of his goods.

Retention of title is often referred to as a 'new' type of security. At the same time, it is also a conventional security, which has its origins in day-to-day business practice. Having said this, retention of ownership/property has long been contested from a judicial perspective, since it was seen as being contradictory to the logic of the contract: it prevented execution of the essential principle of the transfer of ownership on the basis of a simple agreement (*solo consensu*).

The European Directive of 29 June 2000 on the combating of late payment in commercial transactions was the first official recognition of the principle of retention of title. At the same time, each member state also has the right to maintain its own national system, running in parallel. This complicates the situation from a legal point of view (international private law). The legal validity of retention of ownership, in particular the conditions under which it was brought about, is determined by contract law (*lex contractus*). But the real problem with this type of security is its legal enforceability with regard to third parties. If the right of ownership retention is created legitimately, its effect with regard to third parties is governed in principle by the law of the country where the goods in question are located (*lex rei sitae*) or the law of the country where the bankruptcy/insolvency was declared (*lex concursus*), if there is concurrence.

2.2 UNITED KINGDOM.

In the United Kingdom retention of title clauses are permitted by section 19 of the Sale of Goods Act 1979, confirmed by the Court of Appeal in the Romalpa case (1979; Aluminium Industrie Vaassen BV (Netherlands) vs. Romalpa Aluminium Ltd. (UK): Vaassen claimed retention of title against Romalpa). This last case is very important, and retention of title clauses are also called Romalpa clauses, because the case established the legal principle.

There are certain fundamental principles common to all effective Romalpa clauses. There must be a clear intention to retain title in the goods until full payment is received – which is especially important if the goods can be paid for in instalments. The seller should also create a right (or licence) to enter the property of the buyer without notice to physically remove the goods from the buyers' premises.

In order to effectively achieve this, the seller should stipulate that the goods are clearly labelled as being the property of the seller and must be stored away from other goods, thereby making retrieval easier. The buyer should also be under an obligation to ensure that the goods are adequately insured against all usual risks, in the event that anything should happen to them while title remains with the seller.

In some cases, the goods may be sold on to a third party before title has passed. In this event the seller can attempt to demand that the proceeds of the sale are kept separately and held in trust by the buyer for the seller. However, *case law* on this issue makes successful implementation of such clauses far from certain. Similarly, if the goods sold are incorporated into other goods (such as fabric in a garment), then the seller's right to recover can only be realised through part ownership of the finished goods or recovery of some of the proceeds of sale. The difficulty with both of these purportedly enhanced rights is that they may go beyond retention of title and create a security interest (a charge) instead, which usually requires registration to be effective and does not afford the same protection as a Romalpa clause.

Since title does not pass to the buyer unless the conditions of the clause are met, ownership of the goods remains with the seller. This makes the seller's right to the goods superior to that of any liquidator or administrator of the buyer's assets, putting the seller in a much better position than that of a simple creditor.

GOOD TO KNOW

As long as the three main principles of Romalpa are followed (i.e. a clear, unambiguous reservation of title; the goods are not combined with other goods and are stored separately; and the buyer has a fiduciary obligation to the seller), the seller can be confident of recovering unpaid goods from the clutches of an administrator.

2.3 GERMANY

The right to ownership retention as defined in Germany has had a much larger impact (the largest in Europe) by virtue of its broader scope and interpretation. The owner acquires a kind of derivative right in the event of the sale, processing, incorporation or mixing of his goods. For this reason, the use of ownership retention clauses is almost standard practice in the German business world.

There are a number of different variants:

- The basic variant is the simple retention of title clause (*einfacher Eigentumsvorbehalt*); this relates exclusively to the goods delivered by the supplier to his customer, which are still unprocessed and unpaid.
- The extended retention of ownership clause (*verlängerter Eigentumsvorbehalt*); this extended version ensures that:
  - ownership of the goods remains vested in the supplier, even after alteration or processing, as well as mixing with other movable goods;
  - receivables arising from the advanced reselling of the goods are transferred to the original supplier.

  This is covered by the *Weiterverabeitingsklausel* and the *Vorausabtretungsklausel* respectively.
- The most exhaustive version is the expanded retention of title clause (*erweiteter Eigentumsvorbehalt*); this allows the supplier to retain ownership of the goods until the buyer has fulfilled all his financial obligations towards the supplier, including any other debts not related to these particular goods. It can also include any debts still outstanding in respect of other companies owned or controlled by the buyer (the so-called *Konzernklausel*).

3 Guarantees

A guarantee is an agreement whereby a third party, the guarantor, commits himself unilaterally to carry out an agreed undertaking to the benefit of the creditor, in the event that the debtor himself fails to honour this undertaking.

A distinction needs to be made between guarantees from:

- Third party commercial entities (such as a bank or the parent company of the debtor): these guarantees are mostly unconditional and abstract, because they are not linked to the underlying commercial contract that has to be executed (so that no exceptions based on this contract are possible) and can be claimed at first demand; at an international level, they are ruled by the *International Chamber of Commerce (ICC) Rules on Demand Guarantees*;
- Private persons: these guarantees (known as sureties) are invariably more conditional; they sit alongside the original commercial contract (so that exceptions based on this contract are possible, when the beneficiary, the party for whom the surety has been made, has not fulfilled all of his contractual obligations to the seller); at an international level, the *ICC Rules for Contract Bonds* can apply, especially when financial institutions like insurers intervene.

GOOD TO KNOW

Guarantees from third party commercial entities have a proven track record of effectiveness. Personal guarantees, however, do not.

CHAPTER 12
REINSURANCE

The concept of reinsurance is not widely known amongst the ordinary public, but plays an important role in professional insurance circles. Reinsurers regard credit insurance as a higher-risk activity. In Europe, legislation makes this branch of the insurance sector subject to stringent technical provisions.

1 Definition

The term 'reinsurance' has a number of different meanings in different contexts, but they all essentially involve an agreement whereby the initial insurer transfers to another insurer all or part of the risks he has underwritten. We can therefore say that 'the reinsurer is the insurer of the insurer'.

Within the framework of a global programme, the terms of which are clearly defined and renegotiated each year, the initial insurer transfers to the reinsurer a part of the premium he has received for underwriting the risks of his insured customers. In return, the reinsurer agrees to pay back to the insurer a predetermined proportion of any loss compensation, to which the insurer may become entitled under the terms of his policy. Later recoveries are divided between the insurer and the reinsurer in the same proportion.

GOOD TO KNOW

The reinsurers are therefore the business partners of the insurer, in much the same manner as the shareholders, the insured customers and other stakeholders.

2 Reasons for reinsurance

As mentioned earlier, there are various reasons why an insurer may wish to take out reinsurance cover:

- To protect the insurer's own solvency against:
  - exceptionally large loss compensation claims;
  - unexpected fluctuations in the frequency of compensation claims.

  In this sense, reinsurance can be seen as an alternative means to increase the insurer's available capital.
- To make the insurer's risk portfolio more uniform, by laying off all risks over and above his own retention capacity. Retention is that part of the overall premium and risk that the insurer wishes to retain for himself. A uniform portfolio can be created by applying the law of large numbers and the concept of the mutualisation of risks. This makes it possible to manage risks with the aid of statistical and mathematical models.
- Most insurance sector legislation/regulation is about capital adequacy. To the extent that reinsurance can help in this respect (see earlier), it is a relevant issue. However, there is generally no obligation on an insurance company to re-insure.

3 The advantages of reinsurance

The reinsurance of a part of the insurer's risk portfolio can offer considerable advantages:

1. The stabilisation of his business results (profit/loss). By passing on part of his risks to the reinsurer, the insurer can protect himself against unexpected fluctuations in the number of loss claims. In this way, the reinsurer reduces the insurer's need for additional equity capital, with all the associated (capital) costs that this entails.
2. The increase of his underwriting capacity. The resources of every insurer, no matter how large, are not limitless. The reinsurer allows these resources to be increased, so that the insurer can accept more business, to the benefit of them both.
3. The improvement of his cash-flow. Reinsurance means that the insurer is required to pay fewer claims out of his own liquid resources. As a result, he can restrict the level of funds he needs in the short term. This not only means reduced costs in respect of his short-term credit facilities, but also allows him to invest the surplus funds over a longer period of time at a supe-

GOOD TO KNOW

Through the reinsurance of risks that are above his own coverage capacity, the insurer is better able to meet the requirements of his insured parties. In particular, it allows him to accept larger risks. This creates a greater total volume, with resulting economies of scale, which allows the insurer to reduce his general costs.

rior rate of interest, thereby increasing his financial income. This is one of the key elements in the world of insurance.

4 The technical support he receives from the reinsurer. By virtue of his great knowledge and wide experience of the market, the reinsurer can offer the insurer a variety of useful services, including:
   - the development of refined reinsurance programmes that are better suited to the specific needs of the insurer;
   - the monitoring and price-setting of risks;
   - the training of personnel and the provision of technical reports/documentation.

4 Credit insurers and reinsurance

4.1 THREE METHODS

Reinsurance in the credit insurance sector is generally based on one of three systems:

1 Proportional reinsurance: the transfer of a quota or share of the underwritten risks.
2 Non-proportional reinsurance: the transfer of excess of loss.
3 Facultative reinsurance: the transfer of risk on a specific name.

→ *Quota or share (proportional reinsurance)*

This implies that the insurer transfers an agreed percentage of his risks to the reinsurer. This can vary from insurer to insurer, but, for the bigger credit insurance companies, is usually somewhere between 30 and 50 %. The remaining risks (50 to 70%) are covered directly by the insurer. This is known as the retention. The same principles apply for both commercial and political risks.

→ *Excess of loss (non-proportional reinsurance)*

It may well be that the insurer wishes to protect himself against bad trading years, when even his proportional retention might exceed the desired levels. In this case, he might purchase (additional) cover on an excess of loss basis. For example, he might purchase a 'slice' of cover over and above an agreed ceiling, if the insurer's retention of losses in any one year exceeds that agreed ceiling.

→ *Facultative*

Rather than a treaty, applying to the whole of an insurer's business, this type of reinsurance is available for one-off risks and is negotiated case-by-case. Quota share or excess of loss treaties will refer to the range of covers issued by the insurer. Should he decide to underwrite a single contract risk falling outside the normal range (e.g. a long-term contract), then this is a device he might use.

4.2 WHO PROVIDES REINSURANCE?

There are various options for insurers who wish to take out reinsurance. Firstly, there are a number of very large international reinsurance companies. Worldwide, there are also hundreds of other reinsurance companies, many of whom are seen as 'national champions'. The cession/acceptance of risks between different credit insurers is another alternative. Finally, there are the 'captive' reinsurance companies.

→ *The large reinsurance companies*

There are several large reinsurance companies, operating on a worldwide scale. The most well-known are perhaps Lloyds of London, Munich Re and Swiss Re.

An investment grade (BBB with Standard & Poor's) or better is considered to be an absolute requirement. Even so, many insurers demand an A-rating (or even AA) as a minimum for their reinsurers, so that they can be sure that there is a sufficient margin of safety. To build in added security, the risks are often spread between many different reinsurers.

ATTENTION!

By transferring part of his portfolio, the credit insurer is actually pushing part of the credit risk of the debtor on to the shoulders of the reinsurer. This means that it is important that the reinsurer should have good creditworthiness and an excellent credit rating.

→ *Worldwide reinsurance community*

Reinsurance treaties are agreements between the insurer and a list of reinsurers, who sign up to take on an agreed amount or share of the risk. Very often these reinsurers are not specialists in the credit insurance field. They place their trust in the insurer himself and, very importantly, in the 'lead reinsurer' (for example, Swiss Re or Munich Re) to ensure that all necessary procedures are properly complied with.

→ *Cession/acceptance of risks between credit insurers*

In the past, local credit insurers throughout Europe took small proportional shares in each other's reinsurance treaties. Consequently, they shared in the fortunes or misfortunes of their counterparts in different countries. This practice has tended to fall away, in part because companies are now more international and have started to compete in each other's territories, and in part because the range of risks covered by some companies has become more extensive. (For example, when political risk cover began to be offered, many companies held to their belief that only governmental agencies should be doing this.) Nevertheless, in the major credit insurance companies you will still find, even to this day, a separate profit centre or captive reinsurance company (see below), which uses the capacity of the company to write inwards reinsurance cessions from other insurance companies within its field of credit insurance expertise.

→ *Captive (re)insurance companies*

A 'captive' is an insurance or reinsurance company, created by a commercial, financial or industrial group, which insures or reinsures, either in part or in whole, the risks of the group to which it belongs.

This is a much-used construction in the financial world and is particularly popular with large multinational concerns. When captives are set up in favourable tax and legislative environments (such as Luxemburg, Ireland, Bermuda, Cayman Islands, etc.), they can yield considerable financial rewards.

GOOD TO KNOW

Credit insurers also set up their own captives, so that they have an alternative solution to the scarcity that sometimes exists in the reinsurance market, whilst at the same time keeping the considerable premiums within their own group.

The following credit insurance groups have captives:

- Atradius: Atradius Reinsurance Ltd., located within their International Financial Services Centre in the Dublin Financial Centre (Ireland);
- Euler Hermes: Euler Hermes Reinsurance AG, located in Zurich (Switzerland).

EPILOGUE

Hopefully, it should be clear by now that even though credit insurance at first glance seems to be a fairly technical subject, it is nonetheless relatively easy to acquire some basic insights into how it works. The purpose of this book is to give the reader a picture of the fundamental principles and purposes associated with the credit insurance product. Its contents should have something to offer for everyone in the world of business, whether an insured supplier/seller/creditor or a non-insured customer/buyer/debtor. The former is a customer, the latter a potential prospect.

The insured supplier must realise that the credit insurer, through his key preventative role, supports him in his desire to do business safely and profitably. This does not mean that the credit insurer is prepared to accept each and every risk: that would not make economic sense and quickly lead to his own demise. As a result, he will not approve credit limits for unhealthy companies, although he will always explain the reason for his refusal. To make this possible, the credit insurer places his extensive database at the disposal of the suppliers, which also represents an important form of support for their own internal credit management activities. If we continue this line of thought, we can see that credit insurance is an important tool for the management of the insured customer's working capital. Moreover, credit insurance also prevents the 'domino effect', whereby the insolvency of one major customer could lead to knock-on insolvencies among unpaid suppliers. In similar fashion, credit insurance policies are seen by the banks as a sign of good management, resulting in better internal credit ratings for the companies that possess them. This implies that the 'value' of a credit insurance policy should not simply be measured in terms of the balance between premiums paid and loss compensation received, but needs to be viewed in a much broader perspective. In contrast to other areas of the insurance market, credit insurance demands the active participation of both interested parties, the insurer and the insured, throughout the duration of the policy. This works to the benefit of all concerned in several different areas. Most importantly, it should also be remembered that trade credit insurance does come at a price: the cost of expensive discounts for cash payment proves this point conclusively, and in this context shows that credit insurance premiums are really not expensive at all. That is a key message of this book.

But credit insurance also inevitably has an important public role to play. The impact of supplier credit on trade debtors is huge – a fact proven time and time again during the financial and economic crisis of 2008-2009. Part of the problem in this regard is that there is no direct commercial relationship between the debtor companies and the credit insurers. For this reason, debtors are often wary about providing credit insurers with the information they request – the information that they most urgently need in order to make accurate and up-to-date credit decisions. When this happens, the credit insurer may decide to adopt a restrictive approach to the debtor in question, which can have a negative effect on that debtor's supplier credit, the financing of his working capital and his liquidity. In this manner, the credit insurer almost acts as a kind of invisible bank. The reluctant attitude of the debtor can often be put down to a lack of knowledge and understanding about the purposes of credit insurance. 'Who is this uninvited "outsider", who wants to interfere in the running of my business?' After reading this book, we hope that this question will no longer need to be asked.

Trade credit is a motor of economic growth: money must circulate. But we shouldn't be naïve: in the business world, there are many unscrupulous and untrustworthy poachers at work. In these circumstances, the credit insurer is the economy's gamekeeper and shock-absorber. Long may he continue with this important task.

Reference sources

BASTIN, J., *L'assurance-crédit dans le monde contemporain*, Paris, Editions Jupiter - Editions de Navarre, 1978, 660 p.

BECUE, P. , *Handboek kredietverzekering. De onzichtbare bank*, Antwerp-Oxford, Intersentia, 2008, 878 p.

Abbreviations

AA	*Annual aggregate*
AFL	*Aggregate first loss*
AGM	*Annual general meeting*
BU	*Business unit*
CDO	*Collateralised debt obligation*
CRM	*Customer relationship management*
CVA	*Company voluntary arrangement*
DSO	*Days sales outstanding*
ECA	*Expert credit agency*
ECGD	*Export credits guarantee department*
EEFL	*Each and every first loss*
EU	*European Union*
GDP	*Gross domestic product*
ICC	*International Chamber of Commerce*
ICISA	*International Credit Insurance & Surety Association*
IFL	*Integral first loss*
IFRS	*International financial reporting standards*
IPR	*Intellectual property rights*
KPI	*Key performance indicator*
LBO	*Leveraged buy-out*
MEP	*Maximum extension period*
NWC	*Net working capital*
OE	*Operational entity*
OECD	*Organisation for Economic Cooperation and Development*
PD	*Probability of default*
PIT	*Point-in-time*
PMI	*Purchasing manager's index*
RAC	*Risk allocated capital*
ROA	*Return on assets*
ROE	*Return on equity*
SME	*Small and medium-sized enterprises*
UN	*United Nations*
VAT	*Value added tax*
WCR	*Working capital requirement*

Appendix 1: Identification codes in different countries (source: Euler Hermes)

Country	Available identification details	Online codes
Belgium	Company registration or VAT number	BTWBE
Canada	Full name + address + province	No investigation possible via national identification number
Denmark	VAT number	VATDK
Germany	1 For a company: full name and legal form (GMBH, KG, KGAA, GMBH and COKG, OHG, AB, BGB, GBR, EV, EG, EK, VOG) For a sole trader: name of the owner + telephone number (avoid trade names) 2 Full street name + house number (always apply for limits on the address of the company headquarters) 3 Postcode (5 numbers) 4 Place of abode (avoid post box addresses (postfach – pf); these are difficult to check). 5 Trade register number: HR + 1 letter (A, B or G) + listed numbers	No investigation possible via national identification number
Finland	Trade register: RC	RC
France	SIREN number (VAT number minus the first two numbers = SIREN number) If no SIREN number: correct name, address and postcode	SIREN number

Gibraltar	Registration number	CN
Greece	Registration number	RN
Great Britain	*Registered firm (Ltd, Plc, etc):* CRO (Company Registered Office) *Non-registered firm:* No company number (CN) Very important: correct name (trade name and official name), name of owners, VAT number, telephone number, main address (very important to have all these elements)	CRO
Ireland	Company number (CN)	CN
Iceland	Registration number	RN
Italy	CODICE FISCALE: fiscal code with the Italian Ministry of Finance	COFIS
Luxemburg	IBLC = VAT number	IBLC
Netherlands	KvK number (registration number with the Kamer van Koophandel (KvK = Chamber of Commerce). If no KvK number: correct name (trade name and official name), name of owners + full address and postcode	KVK
Norway	Registration number	RN
Austria	Firmenbuchnummer (FN = company registration number)	RC
Portugal	Registration number	NIPC
Spain	CIF/NIF (CIF: companies / NIF: sole traders)	CIF
Czech Republic	VAT number (ICO)	ICO

Sweden	According to legal form: * Limited Cy: registration number, of which the first three numbers are 556 (National Patent and Registration Office) * General liability partnerships * Limited liability partnerships: registration number starting with 9 or 916 (county council trade registers) * Incorporated associations: registration number starting with 7 (county council trade registers) * Single proprietorship: registration number + date of birth of owner (county council registers)	RN
Switzerland	Full name, address and canton	No investigation possible via national identification number
USA	Full name, address and state	No investigation possible via national identification number

Appendix 2: Registration/proposal form for a prospect (source: Euler Hermes)

Proposal for Credit Insurance Policy

EULER HERMES

1 Applicant Information

This form can be completed for commercial or commercial and political risk credit insurance policies. All information provided will be treated in the strictest of confidence.

Applicant Business Name

Trading Style: Company/Firm/Owner (delete as appropriate)

Business Address (for all correspondence) Town

Postcode Country

Contact Name

Position in Company

National ID No. (Co. Registration No. in U.K.) VAT No.

Tel. No. Fax No. email.

Joint Applicants YES ❑ NO ❑ (if yes please ensure the information on all applicants is provided – using a separate sheet if necessary)

Have you been declined for Credit Insurance in the last 3 years? YES ❑ NO ❑

if yes please provide details

2 Description of Business

Types of goods/services provided ____________________

To what trade sector are they sold/provided? ____________________

Please specify whether you are a manufacturer, distributor, agent or merchant? (state which) ____________________

Other (please specify) ____________________

NOTES

Please note for sections 3-10 Turnover Figures and debtor balances should exclude direct sales to associated and subsidiary companies, as well as Government Departments, Public Authorities and Nationalised undertakings except where public buyer default cover is required.

3 Turnover (please state currency if not Sterling)

Countries Note: Please attach schedule if insufficient	Estimated Annual Turnover (excluding VAT)	Maximum Exposure at any one time	Approx No. of accounts	Normal Terms and method of payment including credit period	Commercial cover required	Requirements for Export only	
						Commercial & Political Risk cover	Public Buyer Default

Do you sell to countries not included above? YES ❑ NO ❑
(if yes, please state countries, turnover and reason for their exclusion)

Third Country Risk – Do you despatch goods or provide services to, or obtain payment from, any country other than your or the customer's country? YES ❑ NO ❑

If yes, please provide details ____________________

Please continue details on a separate sheet if necessary

A company of Allianz

1

4 Past Trading Experience In the event of an abnormal loss in any year an explanation of circumstances must be attached.

Financial Year Ending (mm/yy)	Turnover excluding VAT (state currency if not sterling)	Aggregate bad debt losses*	Number of bad debts	Largest Individual bad debt	Company name and country of largest bad debt
Year to date					

*State true bad debts - not bad debts written off in that year

5 Active Accounts – Debtor Analysis Please indicate the number of debtors, by size of debt and indicate percentage of total turnover/debtor balance in each band. State currency if not sterling.

Outstanding debtor balance at any one time	Number of debts	% of Total *Turnover/ Debtor Balance	Debt (balance outstanding at any one time)	Number of debts	% of Total *Turnover/ Debtor Balance
Up to £1,000			£25,001 -£50,000		
£1,001 - £2,500			£50,001 -£100,000		
£2,501 - £5,000			£100,001 -£500,000		
£5,001 - £10,000			£500,001 -£1,000,000		
£10,001 - £25,000			£1,000,000+		

*Delete as appropriate

Date of analysis / /

6 Total of Debtors Balances

Accounting period ending month 3	£	Accounting period ending month 9	£
Accounting period ending month 6	£	Accounting period ending month 12	£

Are there any seasonal peaks in your business? YES ❑ NO ❑ If yes, when?

Aged Debtor Analysis as at (date):	£
Current – not yet due	£
1-30 days overdue	£
31-60 days overdue	£
61-90 days overdue	£
more than 90 days overdue	£

(Names of any accounts which are seriously overdue will be required in section 8)

7 Credit Management

a) Who is responsible for the overall credit control system?

Name

Position

b) If credit control is **not** centralised at the address given on page 1 please give full address details here:

c) Are credit limits established on individual customers? YES ❑ NO ❑

d) On what basis is a specific credit limit established? (financial or otherwise)

Status Reports YES ❑ NO ❑ Agency Name:

Audited / management accounts YES ❑ NO ❑

Other Sources used (e.g. trading experience) please state

Are regular personal visits made to the customer? If yes, who makes such visits? YES ❑ NO ❑ ❑ WHO:

e) Are you able to prepare from your records a retrospective trading history for each buyer by Calendar month?

YES ❑ NO ❑

f) How often is credit information updated? (please tick box)

3 months ❑ 6 months ❑ 9 months ❑ 12 months ❑ Longer ❑ please specify____________

g) How often is a credit limit reviewed? Who does this?

h) What information do you use when reviewing the credit limit?

i) Do you refer to the state of the account before authorising?

Acceptance of order YES ❑ NO ❑ Despatch/Delivery YES ❑ NO ❑

j) How many days after due date do you normally...

	No. of days	Who has the authority to take action?
..stop futher supplies?	________	________________
..take collection action?	________	________________
..take legal action?	________	________________

k) Please give full details of your procedures for collecting overdue debts. ________________

If you use a Collection Agency, please specify which company.

l) Do you have Retention of Title incorporated into your contract? YES ❑ NO ❑

If yes, state whether "Specific invoice" ❑ or "All monies" ❑

8 Overdue Accounts

If you have any accounts which are more than 60 days past due date or you are aware of any circumstances where the buyer is or maybe unable to meet their payment obligations with you, please give details as below. **If not please state none.**

Name, Address & Country	Amount Outstanding	Original due date	Reason for overdue and action taken
National ID No.			
National ID No.			
National ID No.			
National ID No.			
National ID No.			

9 Special Terms of Payment

If you have any accounts where you have agreed to terms that differ from your normal terms of payment, please detail the name and address of the account, the terms agreed, the credit limit and the turnover involved.

Name, Address & Country	National ID No.	Payment Terms Agreed	Credit Limit	Annual Turnover

10 Additional Information

a) Is your business involved in any of the following?

	YES	NO	(if yes please give details and advise estimated annual turnover)
Consignment stocks	❑	❑	
Long term contracts	❑	❑	
Paid-when-paid contracts	❑	❑	
Retentions	❑	❑	
Work in progress	❑	❑	(if yes please complete a separate work in progress questionnaire)
b) Do you have an existing credit insurance policy?	❑	❑	(if yes, state current insurer and renewal date)
Do you have invoice discounting / factoring arrangements?	❑	❑	(if yes, please give details)

11 Cross section of your current customers

Name, Address and Country	National ID No.	*Credit Limit Required (state currency if not sterling)
1		
2		
3		
4		
5		
6		
7		
8		
9		
10		
11		
12		
13		
14		
15		
16		
17		
18		

*Credit Limit = maximum amount outstanding at any one time.

12 Declaration and Data Use

I/We, including any joint applicants, declare and warrant to you that the information given in this Proposal and any attachments is in all respects true and accurate and that we have disclosed all information which might influence underwriters in fixing the premium and accepting the risk.

Our disclosure and warranty does not limit any legal obligation or duty upon us at common law or otherwise to disclose to you all material facts and circumstances, and to act with utmost good faith at all times. I/We accept that this Proposal shall be the basis of the contract between us and will form part of any Policy issued.

Privacy Notice and Consent

We acknowledge and agree that Euler Hermes UK may:

(a) process personal data provided by us, including personal data relating to the partners, directors, shareholders and employees of our business and our customers ("relevant data"), for the purpose of carrying out credit insurance and any associated activities, including risk assessment and debt collection ("relevant activities");

(b) transfer relevant data to any company or branch within the Euler Hermes Group and to responsible third parties (including entities outside the European Economic Area where necessary), for the purpose of carrying out relevant activities;

(c) disclose relevant data to and use information from credit reference agencies for credit risk assessment and identification purposes;

(d) retain relevant data for a reasonable time after termination of our policy or rejection of this application, for audit purposes; and

(e) except where the box below is ticked, contact us regarding Euler Hermes products and services, which may be of interest to us in writing, electronically, by phone or other means.

Please tick this box if you do not wish your personal data to be used for marketing purposes. ☐

We agree that you may share our personal data with fraud prevention agencies, regulatory bodies and other law enforcement agencies (including the police) for prevention and detection of fraud and money laundering. We understand that if we have given false or misleading information and you identify fraud, you will identify this in your records and may retain such records for a reasonable period.

We confirm that we have obtained the consent of and are authorised by all relevant individuals to provide their personal data to Euler Hermes UK and to permit the processing of such data as set out in this notice.

Further information on how Euler Hermes UK may process personal data, and other data protection issues, can be found in the Data Protection Guide contained in your policy documentation.

Authorised Signature of Applicant(s) Date

Printed Name of Signatory

Position within the Business

Company Stamp (if available/applicable)

(if there is no stamp, please write "duly authorised to sign for and on behalf of ....the Business Name").

A copy of our most recent financial report and accounts is enclosed ☐

To be completed by Broker/Euler Hermes UK Business Centre

Broker/Euler Hermes UK Business Centre__________

Name __________

Address __________

____

Euler Hermes UK
1 Canada Square
London
E14 5DX
Tel : +44 (0)20 7512 9333
Fax : +44 (0)20 7512 9186
www.eulerhermes.co.uk